## TWAYNE'S WORLD AUTHORS SERIES (TWAS)

*The purpose of TWAS is to survey the major writers
—novelists, dramatists, historians, poets, philosophers,
and critics—of the nations of the world. Among the
national literatures covered are those of Australia,
Canada, China, Eastern Europe, France, Germany,
Greece, India, Italy, Japan, Latin America, New Zea-
land, Poland, Russia, Scandinavia, Spain, and the
African nations, as well as Hebrew, Yiddish, and
Latin Classical literatures. This survey is comple-
mented by Twayne's United States Authors Series
and English Authors Series*

*The intent of each volume in these series is to present
a critical-analytical study of the works of the writer;
to include biographical and historical material that
may be necessary for understanding, appreciation,
and critical appraisal of the writer; and to present all
material in clear, concise English—but not to vitiate
the scholarly content of the work by doing so.*

*TWAYNE'S WORLD AUTHORS SERIES*

*A Survey of the World's Literature*

Sylvia E. Bowman, Indiana University

**GENERAL EDITOR**

# SPAIN

Gerald Wade, Vanderbilt University

**EDITOR**

## Lope de Vega

*( TWAS 28 )*

# Lope de Vega

By FRANCIS C. HAYES

*University of Florida*

Twayne Publishers, Inc.   ::   New York

Library of Congress Catalog Card Number: 67–19352

A LA MEMORIA DE HOWARD, MAX, LAURA S. Y JULIUS F. HAYES

# Preface

LOPE de Vega (1562–1635), the most prolific playwright who
ever lived, had eminent contemporaries at home and abroad.
Some of these contemporaries were Christopher Marlowe, Ben
Jonson, William Shakespeare, Pierre Corneille, Cervantes, and
Calderón de la Barca—to name the greatest. Lope lived during
the most exuberantly productive period of Spain's history, an
age generally called in Spanish "el siglo de oro" (the Golden
Age). Its duration was roughly 1550–1680. Today in Spain, by
common consent, Lope is considered to be Spain's most illustrious
dramatist. A Nobel Prize winner, Jacinto Benavente, for example,
was an impetuously ardent champion of Lope, whom he placed
above all dramatists, not excepting Shakespeare: "I, for my part,
consider our Lope far superior to Shakespeare, Corneille, Racine,
and Molière, and I hate to think how vastly exalted his name
and fame might have been had any other nation than Spain
(Spaniards being thought of as poor relations) borne a Lope de
Vega." [1]

F. C. Sáinz de Robles, distinguished contemporary Spanish
critic and editor, approaches Lope on his knees, metaphorically,
much as a devout Catholic might approach the statue of a saint.
Sáinz de Robles is one of several of the most recent biographers
of Lope writing in Spanish, and his admiration for the playwright
verges on veneration: "Lope measures a height of twenty meters,"
says Sáinz, "like those seated, rigid Rameses and Amenophises
which adorn the unroofed columned halls of Luxor and Karnak.
In order to believe in a Lope of normal stature, one must con-
template him from a distance . . . as one must do the Pharaohs.
. . . It is unthinkable that flesh and blood, bone and nerve,
sensation and feeling, idea and ideal . . . could contain an
ordinary soul like the rest of us. . . ." Continuing with several

pages of encomium, thoroughly mixing in his god-and-sea metaphors, Sáinz finally claims mythdom for Lope, exclaiming, "I
throw myself precipitously into the sea which is Lope's soul.
. . . Since one must approach myths with fact or with faith, I
approach him with faith. I believe in Lope, Spanish literature's
greatest myth." [2]

Another Lope devotee, José Martínez Ruiz, one of Spain's
most lyrical and evocative essayists, better known under the
pseudonym of "Azorín," also extols Lope with extravagant praise.
"Lope is the real world. Everything is to be found in Lope. The
four corners of the earth . . . and the nations of Europe in
particular; and Greek antiquity; and Roman antiquity; and Chris-
tianity; and the lives of saints; and the most haloed heroes in
the universe; and the mountains; and the rivers; and the forests;
and the cities. Lope's genius has fluttered around over everything
on earth. Neither time nor space has held secrets for him. His
strength is pliant, light, smooth: an immense poet's strength,
prodigious, titanic, yet appearing as simple as a child's." [3] Azorín
even elevates Lope beyond good and evil: "Lope, driven by
personal hunger, places himself in one leap outside his contemporary moral climate. His contemporaries inhabited one
moral region and he another." [4] Azorín had in mind that Lope's
galloping eroticism always outpaced his Apostolic Roman Catholic conscience.

The common man in Spain also manifested his devotion to
Lope. To honor his four hundredth birthday in 1962, eighty
thousand spectators gathered in a Madrid stadium to hear interpretations of passages from some fifteen of his plays as presented by *aficionados,* and the press coverage in the Hispanic
world was on a par with the huge size of the gathering. This
honor was only one of many paid Lope. The entire Spanish-
speaking world joined in countless acts of homage, before, during,
and following his quadricentennial year, with performances of
his plays, scholarly addresses to large assemblies, publications
of articles and books (including several new biographies), adaptation of plays to television, and even eulogies to crowds in the
streets of Madrid.

It seems strange that this dramatist who excites such admiration and wonder in his own country has aroused relatively so

little interest in the English-speaking world. It has been more than a century and a half since Lord Holland published *The Life of Lope de Vega* in London, in 1807. Then almost a century went by before Hugo Albert Rennert published *The Life of Lope de Vega,* in 1904, in Glasgow—reprinted in New York in 1937.[5]

My purpose in writing this book, therefore, is to offer to the English-speaking reader an account of Lope de Vega and his works based upon my own reading, and, naturally, upon the labors and researches of many others.

This book is intended for everyone interested in Spanish drama—from the general reader just breaking new (Spanish) literary grounds, to the Lope specialist (*lopista*) who revels in reading again things he already knows by heart.

Some readers may notice the absence of a chapter on the history of Spain of the time of Lope de Vega. To deal with the history of this period would go beyond the scope of this volume and lead into regions already well mapped out by historians of Spain in easily obtained history books. One of the most readable is John A. Crow, *Spain: The Root and the Flower,* New York: Harper and Row, 1963; see chapters six through nine.

FRANCIS C. HAYES

*University of Florida*

# Contents

# Acknowledgments

I wish to thank the Graduate School of the University of Florida for a grant which supplemented my income sufficiently in 1961 to enable me to do a part of the research on this volume in Europe. For permission to quote, thanks go to Hill and Wang, Inc., publishers of *Lope de Vega—Five Plays*, newly translated by Jill Booty, edited with introduction by R. D. F. Pring-Mill, New York: A Mermaid Dramabook, 1961. For generous and indispensable editorial assistance and for indexing, thanks go to Mrs. Rita Barlow of Gainesville. For many kindnesses thanks are also due several members of the staff of the Biblioteca Nacional in Madrid—with a special word of gratitude to the elderly pages who laboriously brought countless volumes to my desk from the library stacks.

# Chronology

Lope's biographers are frequently at variance with one another in the matter of dates. The dates given for the plays listed below are for the most part approximate dates of composition and are based on the Morley-Bruerton *Chronology of Lope de Vega's Plays*.[1]

| | |
|---|---|
| 1562 | Birth of Lope, St. Lope's Day (December 12), at 48 Calle Mayor in Madrid.[2] Baptized in the church of San Miguel de los Octoes, no longer standing. |
| 1572 | Lope begins study of Latin and Spanish with the novelist Vicente Espinel. |
| 1574– 1576 | Lope attends a Jesuit school. May have taken part in school plays. According to his own statement, he wrote his first play at the age of twelve. |
| 1576 | Employed in the household of Bishop Jerónimo Manrique de Lara; attends the University of Alcalá de Henares until 1578 (?). |
| 1578 | Death, in Madrid, of his father, August 17. Lope leaves the service of Bishop Manrique de Lara; enters service of Don Pedro de Dávila, Marquis of Las Navas. |
| 1580 | To the University of Salamanca (?). |
| 1583 Age 21 | Enlists in the armed forces sent to quell a rebellion in the Azores. On return to Madrid begins love affair with Elena Osorio. |
| *ca.* 1586 | Attends the Academy of Mathematics of Juan Bautista Labaña. |
| *ca.* 1587– 1588 Age 26 | Break with Elena Osorio (*"Dorotea"*). Lope circulates slanderous verse about Elena; is convicted for malicious libel. Probable date of composition of *La Dorotea;* published much later (1632). |

1588 May 10, Lope marries by proxy Isabel de Urbina, age 17; he leaves (May 29) almost certainly to join the Invincible Armada via Lisbon; probably composes *The Beauty of Angélica* (*La hermosura de Angélica*) on this expedition. Moves to Valencia with new wife, Isabel de Urbina.

1590 Enters the service of the Marquis of Malpica in Toledo for a few months; next serves the Duke of Alba. *The Valencian Shore* (*El Grao de Valencia*), play, 1589–90 (?).

1594 Death of wife, Isabel de Urbina, in childbirth. *The Dancing Master* (*El maestro de danzar*), play, 1594.

1596 Leaves Duke of Alba's service. *The Knights* (*Commanders*) *of Córdoba* (*Los comendadores de Córdoba*), play, 1596–98; *Marriage in Death* (*El casamiento en la muerte*), play, 1595–97.
Age 34

1598 Probable beginning of intimate relations with Micaela de Luján ("Camila Lucinda"), wife of Diego Díaz, actor. *The Life and Death of King Wamba* (*La vida y muerte del rey Bamba*), play, 1597–98; *Columbus's Discovery of the New World* (*El Nuevo Mundo descubierto por Cristóbal Colón*), play, 1598–1603.

1598 On April 25 Lope marries Juana de Guardo, daughter of a rich meat-and-fish wholesaler. Outbreak of literary quarrel between Lope and Luis de Góngora. Lope publishes *Drake the Pirate* (*La Dragontea*) vituperating Sir Francis Drake; *The Arcadia* (*La Arcadia*), a pastoral novel written in 1590. *The Beautiful Mismatched Wife* (*La bella malmaridada*), play.

1599 With the Marquis of Sarriá to Valencia to attend double royal wedding. Published *Isidro* (*El Isidro*), honoring patron saint of Madrid; *The Araucans Conquered* (*El arauco domado*), play, 1598–1603; *The Valencian Widow* (*La viuda valenciana*), play, 1595–1603.

1602 Publishes *The Beauty of Angelica* (*La hermosura de Angélica*) and *Rhymes* (*Rimas*). *The Assassinated Prince* (*El príncipe despeñado*), play, 1602; *The Knight From Illescas* (*El caballero de Illescas*), play,

|        | 1602; *Remedy For Misfortune* (*El Remedio en la Desdicha*), play, 1595–1602. |
|--------|-------------------------------------------------------------------------------|
| 1604   | First volume of collection of *Plays* (*Comedias*); volumes will appear periodically until 1647, totaling 25, each with twelve plays. *Charles V in France* (*Carlos V en Francia*), play. |
| 1604   | Publishes *The Pilgrim in his Own Country* (*El peregrino en su partia*), a novel, in Seville; volume includes incomplete listing of plays to 1604; to Toledo, taking both wife and mistress, Micaela de Luján, setting up two households. *Saint Isidro of Madrid* (*San Isidro de Madrid*), play, 1604–06 (?). |
| 1605   | Enters employ of don Luis Fernández de Córdoba, sixth Duke of Sessa; will serve approximately 26 years as Sessa's secretary. |
| 1606   | *The Grand Duke of Russia* (*El gran duque de Moscovia*), play, 1606; *The Lure of Fenisa* (*El anzuelo de Fenisa*), play, 1604–1606 (?). |
| 1609 Age 47 | Publishes the poem *Jerusalem Regained* (*Jerusalén conquistada*), an imitation of Tasso's *Gerusalemme Liberata* (1581). Defends himself from Aristotelian critics with *The New Art of Play Writing* (*Arte nuevo de hacer comedias*). Enters the Congregation of Slaves of the Holy Sacrament. *The Iron Tonic of Madrid* (*El acero de Madrid*), play, 1608–12; *Peribáñez*, 1609–12. |
| 1610   | In Madrid with his second wife, Juana de Guardo, and family. *Seductive Esther* (*La hermosa Ester*), play, April 5; *The Stunning Beauty* (*La niña de plata*), play, 1610–12. |
| 1611   | Publishes *Devotional Soliloquies of a Soul to its God* (*Soliloquios amorosos de un alma a su Dios*) and *The Shepherds of Bethlehem* (*Los pastores de Belén*), poems. *Count Fernando González* (*El conde Fernán González*), play; *Barlaam and Jehoshaphat* (*Barlán y Josafá*), play; *The Farmer's House Is His Castle* (*El villano en su rincón*), play. |
| 1612   | Publishes *Sacred Prose and Verse* (*Prosas y versos divinos*). *The Sheepwell* (*Fuente Ovejuna*), play, |

1612–14 (?); *The Tranquility of Kings* (*Las paces de los reyes*), play, 1610–12.

1613 Death of wife, Juana de Guardo, at birth of Feliciana, August 4. *The Dog in the Manger* (*El perro del hortelano*), play, 1613–15; *The Birth of Christ* (*El nacimiento de Cristo*), play, 1613–15.

1613 Lope begins love affair with Jerónima de Burgos ("la señora Gerada"), actress often known as "la Roma." *Miss Simpleton* (*La dama boba*), April 28.

1614 Lope becomes a priest; says his first mass on May 24.
Age 51 *Arcadia* (*La Arcadia*), play, 1614.

1616 *Sowing In Good Earth* (*El sembrar en buena tierra*), play, 1616.

ca. 1617 Begins intimate relations with Marta de Nevares Santoya ("Amarilis"), unhappy young wife of business man Roque Hernández de Ayala.

1617 Antonia Clara is born to Lope and Marta de Nevares.

1620 Lope vainly seeks the position of Royal Historian. *A Certainty For a Doubt* (*Lo cierto por lo dudoso*), 1620–24; *The Knight of Olmedo* (*El caballero de Olmedo*), 1620–25, both plays.

1621 Publication of *The Nightingale* (*La Filomena*), a miscellany of prose and verse, and *Andromeda* (*La Andrómeda*), based on the tale of Perseus; *The King the Greatest Alcalde* (*El mejor alcalde, el Rey*), play, 1620–23.

1623 *The Star of Seville* (*La Estrella de Sevilla*), of doubtful authorship.[3]

1624 *The Marquis of Las Navas* (*El marqués de las Navas*), play, 1624. *La Circe*, a poem, with a miscellany of stories and epistles.

1627 Pope Urban VIII honors Lope with membership in the Order of Saint John of Jerusalem and the honorary title of "Doctor of Theology" and "Friar." *The Tragic Crown* (*La corona trágica*), long poem concerning Mary Stuart. *The Girl With the Pitcher* (*La moza de cántaro*), play, before 1627.

1630 Publishes *The Laurel of Apollo and other verse* (*Laurel de Apolo, con otras rimas*): praise in verse of some 300 poets.

1631 *Punishment Without Revenge* (*El castigo sin venganza*), play, August 1; *St. John's Night* (*La noche de San Juan*), play, 1631.

1632 Publishes *Dorothy* (*La Dorotea*), a largely autobiographical dialogue in prose and scattered verse, probably written in 1588. Death of Marta de Nevares.

1633 *Amarilis. Egloga.* Pastoral poem partly autobiographical; "Amarilis" Lope's name for Marta de Nevares.

1634 *Human and Divine Rhymes* (*Rimas humanas y divinas*), published under pseudonym of Tomé de Burguillos: a miscellany of verse, some serious, some burlesque. *Belisa's Bizarre Valor* (*Las bizarrías de Belisa*), play; *The Battle of Cats* (*La gatomaquia*), mock-epic poem. Last play probably (*A King's Greatest Virtue*) *La mayor virtud de un rey.*

1635 *Filis. Egloga.* Mainly the veiled expression of Lope's grief and bitterness at the abduction of his daughter, Antonia Clara, called Filis in this poem. Lope, now 73, scourges himself every Friday, repeatedly repents his misdeeds; dies August 27; funeral a national affair; buried in the Church of Saint Sebastian in Madrid, no longer standing. Some years later his remains thrown into common grave.

1637 *Eclogue to Claudio* (*Egloga a Claudio*). Autobiographical and bibliographical; the nostalgic memories of Lope in old age; much self-analysis and self-criticism. Contains Lope's statement that he had written more than one hundred plays within a twenty-four hour period each and that the total number ascended to 1,500 plays.

# CHAPTER 1

## *The Man Lope de Vega*

### I  *Lope's Life and Career in Brief*

LOPE Félix de Vega Carpio (1562–1635) is the most prolific
poet-playwright of all time and is generally ranked first in
Spanish dramatic literature. He was a most turbulent spirit. However soberly one speaks of his life, literary or personal, the result
seems tinged with sensationalism. He was extraordinarily precocious, and, it must be agreed, something of a juvenile delinquent. He claims that he wrote his first play (in verse) when
he was twelve. Before his death at seventy-three he had written
so many plays that neither he nor anyone knew the exact number.
His first biographer, Juan Pérez de Montalbán, who was also a
close (and overly enthusiastic) friend, set the figure at eighteen
hundred, excluding the religious plays or *autos sacramentales.*
Lope himself claimed fifteen hundred but we know he was on
occasion inattentive, even casual, in his use of figures. A more
trustworthy inventory would probably list between seven hundred and eight hundred titles. His collected plays in 1647
(twelve years after his death) numbered twenty-five volumes.
He tapped almost every literary source known to seventeenth-
century Spain and wrote enough drama, considered quantita-
tively, for a whole nation of playwrights. He created between
seventeen thousand and twenty thousand characters, although
thousands were repeated, formula-fashion. Even so, these figures
only partly tell the story, for he also wrote numerous volumes
of mock and classical epics, lyric verse, one-act religious plays,
ballads, a novelized autobiography, and prose stories, besides
thousands of letters written in his capacity as secretary consecutively to a number of noblemen, with one of whom, the
Duke of Sessa, he held a position off and on for twenty-six years
beginning in 1605. According to Ezra Pound, Lope was like ten
brilliant minds inhabiting one body, and attempts to enclose

[ 17 ]

him in any formula is like trying to make one pair of boots fit a centipede.[1]

Most scholars are agreed that Lope de Vega's excessive productiveness was his worst shortcoming. He himself for years considered his plays outside the domain of art. He freely admitted, in his *New Way to Write Plays in Our Time* (1609), that he wrote for the multitude. Only fairly late in life did he consider publishing his plays, for he said that his chief motive in writing them was an eager, wearying quest for money, always liberally spent and constantly in short supply.

The material out of which Lope built his plays is varied. Frequently used are the young men and young women of his day, especially in his cape-and-sword plays. The young men, an indispensable part of whose dress was a razor-edged sword, were unusually highbred, gentlemanly, hotheaded, courageous, extravagant in the use of lyrical compliments to women, arrogantly and defiantly proud, and punctiliously slavish to the dictates of the current face-saving code, or *pundonor*. The women were beautiful, gay, energetic, patient, quick to sacrifice, heroic, and without "rights" in the modern sense. They, too, were supposed to live strictly by the honor code, and vigilant fathers and brothers tried (usually unsuccessfully, if we believe the *comedia*) to see that they did. Generally his women characters are superior to the men. All classes and types of people, from kings and queens to peasants, abound in the vast Lopean repertory. The enigmatic exception here is the character of the mother, who rarely appears on any seventeenth-century Spanish stage either in Lope's plays or in anyone else's.

Almost invariably Lope included comic characters, called *graciosos,* both male and female, to amuse with parodies on the actions and the lines of the principals, and to delight with interpolated anecdotes, tales, jokes, and above all, puns. These comedians were nearly indispensable for the success of any Spanish play, humorous or tragic.

An exhaustive study of Lope's genius for portraying graphically the whole society around him is found in a large volume by Ricardo del Arco y Garay, *Spanish Society in the Dramatic Works of Lope de Vega* (*La sociedad española en las obras dramáticas de Lope de Vega,* Madrid, 1941). But, in addition

to Lope's use of social materials, much of his subject matter
came from lives of saints and kings, pastoral tales, mythology,
the Bible, Spanish history, current events, the New World (occasionally), and folklore (traditions, legends, ballads, epic poems,
folk tales, proverbs). A few titles of some of Lope's best-known
plays are *The Sheep Well* (*Fuenteovejuna*), *The King the Best
Mayor* (*El mejor alcalde, el rey*), *The Dog in the Manger* (*El
perro del hortelano*), and *Miss Simpleton* (*La dama boba*).
Music and dancing were frequent and stage machinery was
generally minimized, though varied and at times sensational.
For example, Saint Isidro in one scene of the trilogy based on
his life was grasped by an angel by the hair of the head and
transported at supersonic speed across continents.

The vastness of the quantity of Lope's dramatic work gives
rise to comparative neglect of his lyric poetry by scholars. Yet
he would easily be placed among the best lyric poets of Spain
even if he had never written a play. He appears in all Spanish
anthologies of poetry. Some of the titles of his collected poems
are *Verse* (*Rimas*, 1604); *Sacred Verse* (*Rimas sacras*, 1614);
*Verse Human and Divine* (*Rimas humanas y divinas* . . . ,
1634). Throughout his drama he was lavish with sonnets and
a variety of other verse. "Versification," he wrote in *New Way
to Write Plays in Our Time,* "should be carefully accommodated
to the subject treated. . . . When the King speaks, imitate as
best you can the royal gravity. . . . The speech of lovers should
be passionate, so that it carries away the listener; depict soliloquies in such a way that the actor is wholly transformed, and
so transforms the audience. . . ."

Perhaps the most unsubstantial part of Lope's work is his narrative poetry. *Drake the Pirate* (*La Dragontea*, 1598), for example,
is an unrestrained angry condemnation of Sir Francis Drake, a
work springing from an obsessive collective national hatred of
Drake. *The Tragic Crown, or the Death of Mary Stuart* (*La
corona trágica y la muerte de María Estuardo*, 1627) presents a
Spanish view of the death of Mary Stuart; and Lope somehow
found time in his last years to amuse himself writing a burlesque
epic called *The Battle of the Cats* (*La gatomaquia*).

The standard reference work on Lope in English is H. A.
Rennert, *The Life of Lope de Vega,* New York, 1904; it was re-

printed in 1937 and is still authoritative. It replaced the unreliable biography by Lope's close friend Montalbán, for two centuries the major source of information for subsequent biographers. Montalbán suppressed the episodes in Lope's life that discredit him. The whitewash adhered so tenaciously that a French critic, Adolphe de Puibusque, in 1843 affirmed that "Spain never had an ecclesiastic so zealous for religion nor so strict in his conduct. He lived and died a saint." Twentieth-century scholars, much more knowledgeable through intensive research on Lope's life, present an entirely different man, and are inclined to use the tarbrush, especially in regard to his relationships with women. Twice married, once by proxy, and the father of six legitimate children, he had at least ten illegitimate children born from some ten liaisons. Court records show he was tried and convicted when he was twenty-five for circulating grossly ribald verse about one of his mistresses (Elena Osorio, his "Etna of Love" for some six years) after a violent separation. Elena's mother once quarreled with her over her scandalous love relations with Lope—and in the fray pulled out some of her hair, which Elena promptly sent in a lock to Lope. He wore it on his hat. When the court sentenced him to eight years of exile from Madrid, he disregarded the decree and periodically returned.

Numerous personal comments in his letters to the Duke of Sessa afford an intimate picture of Lope. Both men were deliberately and flagrantly ribald. Lope was sensitive about his age and equivocated when asked about it even when on trial. He went to sea twice, was thoroughly conversant with nautical language, but disliked the ocean. He played the violin. He was annoyed by fans who stopped him in the streets. His flower garden was a joyous recreation and infallible relaxation. He loved cats, kept a houseful, and ran experiments to study their conditioned reflexes over two and a half centuries before Pavlov's similar experiments with dogs. Bullfights, cards, and hunting bored him. He was frequently apprehensive lest he suffer sunstroke. He could be violently jealous and once struck Elena Osorio full in the face for admiring a bullfighter. He was obsequious toward the nobility. Although coming from common Asturian stock, he boasted of his lineage, a current and widespread practice in his day. He aided and counseled the Duke of Sessa in his extramarital affairs. Both relished smut.

On the other side of his ledger, Lope's most unflagging companions were conscience and repentance. His poems of repentance express passionate, unfeigned sorrow. Conscience never let him rest—in the daytime. He repented and confessed weekly but once wrote the Duke of Sessa that one priest in desperation told him "to find himself another confessor." In his old age he whipped himself until the blood tinged the walls of his oratory. He habitually began every page of his writing with a cross, frequently combined with some pious invocation. He recognized all of his children, dedicated one or more poems to each, tried always to be a good provider, and at home was gentle, thoughtful, patient.

Lope's personal life generally had little adverse effect on his prestige. The common man accepted him so enthusiastically that an idolatrous verse, "I believe in Lope de Vega all powerful, poet of heaven and earth . . . ," a parody of Catholic ritual, was circulated and had to be sought out and destroyed by the Inquisition. Lope's picture hung in nearly every home. "It's Lopean" (*"Es de Lope"*) became a synonym for "It's excellent," in reference to anything at all. Royalty accepted him by inviting him to its festivities. The church accepted him by receiving him into the priesthood in 1614. The Spanish Inquisition accepted him by making him one of its judges. He became official censor and granter of the indispensable *nihil obstat,* or imprimatur. Pope Urban VIII in 1627 made him a member of the Order of Saint John of Jerusalem and gave him the honorary title of Doctor of Theology. The military accepted him because he had been once, and probably twice, under fire, first to quell a rebellion in the Azores, the second time (it is generally assumed) in the battle of the Invincible Armada in 1588, in which his brother lost his life. Lope's nine-day funeral was a national affair with over 150 funeral orations, and the cortege that followed him deviated from the customary route to the cemetery to pass the abode of his beloved natural daughter, Sister Marcela, who watched the procession through the iron grating of a cloistered nunnery. Before taking the veil she had been almost his chief consolation.

Lope was buried in a niche of the Church of Saint Sebastian in Madrid, no longer standing, but when the Duke of Sessa stopped paying the rent for the niche, and later the Duke's heirs also refused, Lope's bones were taken to the common grave and intermingled with the bones of the common man whom he had repeatedly exalted in his theater.

One of our most eminent modern critics insists that Lope de Vega was not a man—but a literature.

## II  *Lope and Women: Two Wives, Several Mistresses, Numerous Children, No Descendants*

In the late 1570's young Lope threw himself into the hurly burly life of Madrid with his lusty youthful contemporaries. He schemed to meet the sons of the *gente bien* (best people). These friends *tiraban al monte* (were self-willed, turbulent), as the saying goes. They were boisterous, ready for mischief, on the lookout for deviltry. They went out nightly with Bacchus, Venus, and Mars, were well practiced in how to compliment a woman, to duel, to indulge in smut, to swear roundly—blasphemy in Spanish often involving sex related to one's mother, the Virgin, and the Deity, and being hideous almost beyond the bounds of belief. Anything went to fend off the boredom of youth in the turbulent manner customary with young people of an obstreperous nature. They roamed the streets with their personal bands of musicians and singers. In pursuit of women, they challenged fathers, brothers, husbands, and lovers who might obstruct their path. They had knife fights with the night patrol, engaged in gang warfare, went into debt. They followed one rule with women: make love with haste and forget with dispatch. It ought not to be forgotten that Don Juan, the Great Lover, was created in the Spain of Lope's time.

Though Lope and his friends went to mass every morning, their next stop would be near the Royal Palace to find out the choicest gossip concerning celebrities and to keep it in circulation. In the afternoon they strolled up and down the Prado Boulevard to let themselves be admired by the girls, or they attended the Príncipe or Cruz Theater, where they turned their heads eagerly to flirt with the women crowded by city regulation into the balcony above. At night, Lope and his friends paid suit to ladies married or not, perpetrated practical jokes, jeered at peaceable strangers, had generally a reckless, and, in their nocturnal mood, a hazardously masculine good time.[2]

Such were Lope's juvenile companions, such the kind of life he led on returning to Madrid as a youth to live, not with his mother, but very likely in the less disciplined home of an attractive woman, probably a relative, who, alas, had two teen-age girls, a daughter and a niece. Joaquín Entrambasaguas formerly speculated [3] that one of these girls became Lope's first love, and gave him his first of numerous illegitimate children, and that she entered literary history as Marfisa, the first woman to be named among his onomastic harem. However, in 1941 Entrambasaguas found evidence to the contrary which removed her from Lope de Vega's life and placed her once again back into oblivion.[4]

ELENA OSORIO (DOROTEA), *1583–1587(?)*. Lope the youth had taken out first citizenship papers in the dominion of folly, and when the random element in the universe brought him a chance meeting with Elena Osorio ("Dorotea") in 1583, he qualified fully for naturalization. The mutual effect of their meeting was instantaneous. "I don't know what lucky star was in the ascendancy for lovers when we met, but we had scarcely glanced at each other and spoken when we immediately surrendered to each other." He relished her talents for singing, dancing, and playing several instruments, delighted in her figure, treasured her conversation, her spriteliness, her cleanliness, all of which he describes in his poems to her. He used every literary device to seize upon her beauty and capture it in prose and in verse, searching throughout nature for baroque metaphors, avowing that nature "had distilled all the flowers, aromatic herbs, rubies, corals, pearls, sapphires, and diamonds to confect this drink for the eyes, this toxicant [*sic*] for the ears." He called her his "Etna of Love."

Who was Elena Osorio? She was the daughter of Jerónimo Velázquez, a tiler turned successful actor-director, and his wife Inés Osorio. Elena had a brother, Damián, a prominent Madrid lawyer who specialized in cases concerning the New World. In 1576 she married Cristóbal Calderón, an actor, but the marriage was a failure. Calderón left the coast clear for Lope by his frequent absences from home. He traveled with strolling players in the provinces and even ranged as far as the Spanish colonies in the New World. He certainly presented no hazard to Lope, nor did Elena's parents. Her impresario father evidently listened to gossip about his daughter "with merchant's ears": in Lope de Vega he had in his own household the up-and-coming, most precocious young dramatist in the country, the playwright who was beginning to outpace all playwrights.

Lope loved Elena, as he said, "volcanically." The course of their love was generally like a mountain stream, occasionally smooth, but mostly rapids and falls. He would dream of being her husband; or he would burn with jealousy of her *de jure* husband; or he would rage at her, one time (maybe more) striking her in the face.

So harmoniously did his mind and his hand function together that whatever happened to him might become "instant literature." One finds Lope's mistresses, his friends, his enemies, his times, all recorded in his writings. For example, the sonnets and eclogues which he addressed to his intimate friend, Claudio, constitute a kind of spiritual biography of himself. The ribald verse he wrote in his rage against Elena Osorio, after breaking with her, was so coarse that it landed him first in jail, then into exile. His fury also became "instant verse"; in this instance, the verse boomeranged. *La Dorotea,* a novel in dialogue with interspersed verse, reveals in detail his affair with Elena, ending tumultuously. Lope very likely composed it in the heat of passion, revised it years later, prior to publication in 1632. It clearly manifests the temper of a young man in love rather than that of an old man reminiscing. Few scholars question the autobiographical nature of the story peopled by a cast thinly disguised with pseudonyms, such as "Fernando" for Lope, "Dorotea" for Elena Osorio, and "Teodora" for her mother, Inés.

The immediate cause of his break with Elena Osorio late in 1587 was, according to Lope, her infidelity. She left him for Francisco Perrenot de Granvela, nephew of Cardinal Perrenot de Granvela. Don Francisco lured Elena away with gold and with the connivance of her mother. Very likely Lope himself spent some of this gold, although he knew its source. Even so, losing Elena to a rival whipped him into such a passion that he circulated two filthy poems, one in macaronic Latin verse, the other a ballad in Spanish, ridiculing and vilifying Elena and her family: Jerónimo Velázquez, her father; Inés Osorio, her mother; Dr. Damián Velázquez, her lawyer brother; and other kinfolk.

Elena's family brought suit for criminal libel against Lope, and on December 29, 1587, the police arrested him at the theater (*Corral de las Comedias*) and carried him off to the Royal Jail. Lope was tried for malicious libel, convicted, and sentenced to exile. The court left a full record of the trial which one may read in résumé in Chapter 2 of H. A. Rennert's *Life of Lope de Vega*.

The court records show that Lope jibed that Elena's lawyer brother should not practice law because he was the son of an actor; that he need not work anyway because his promiscuous sister, Elena, was a prosperous prostitute. And Lope termed her father a blundering incompetent producer and a pander. Inés, he defamed as a procuress "who would take Elena anywhere" as a call girl for pay. For good measure, he lampooned a cousin and a niece. Witnesses testified to Lope's guilt, although he denied everything, stoutly maintaining that he and Velázquez, contrary to the charges, were partners and friends, until he (Lope) began to supply a competing producer named Porres with new plays. After the sentence, Lope went to jail, where he remained in a fury for forty-two days continuing loudly to malign the Velázquez family. When his jailer reported these outbursts to the court on February 7, 1588, they doubled the time of banishment. After his departure, he occasionally broke exile to return to Madrid. When Lope's sentence was nearly completed, on March 18, 1595, Elena's father had a change of heart and presented a petition to the court requesting that Lope be pardoned. Some scholars say Velázquez' change of heart was selfishly motivated, that he was hurting for lack of plays by Spain's most successful playwright. Be that as it may, the petition was granted. It was supported by other interested persons, and included a letter from Lope himself in which he says "my offense was a very slight one!" The decree of banishment was lifted.

It seems evident, some scholars to the contrary notwithstanding, that try as he would to forget Elena, Lope could not; evidence points to his loving her through later liaisons and lyricizing her memory to the end of his days.

ISABEL DE URBINA (BELISA), *1588–1594*. MARRIAGE BY PROXY. Possibly on the rebound from his unsavory affair with Elena Osorio, Lope soon married. The girl was Isabel de Urbina (also called Isabel de Alderete), from a prominent Madrid family proud of its ancestry. Her brother, who held high government positions —alderman of Madrid and King-at-Arms to Felipe II and to Felipe III—objected to the marriage. But married they were, although by proxy, May 10, 1588, because Lope remained banished in Valencia; his bride and his proxy took the marriage vows in Madrid. She was seventeen, the tranquil antithesis of the turbulent Elena Osorio. Lope very possibly broke his sentence of exile to spend some days with her, already in his poetry calling her "Belisa" (the anagram of Isabel). His next decision probably took him abruptly away from her: he is thought to have enlisted in His Majesty Felipe II's Invincible Armada. His motivation? María Goyri assigns him speculatively a "foreign-legion" motive: alleviation through desperate action of the pain of heart wounds inflicted by Elena Osorio. The victim of this decision to enlist—and it is almost certain that he did—was his idealistic and ardently enamored bride of a few days, passionately enough in love with him to defy her own family. Her family promptly lodged a charge of abduction against Lope in the Madrid criminal court but as quickly dropped it for reasons still undisclosed. The warmth of Isabel's love cooled not at all, even when Lope left her alone (and probably pregnant) to face the unpleasantness of her family's opposition.

Lope is believed to have gone to Lisbon to await embarkation with the Armada on May 29. With him went his brother, Juan, and four cronies of dubious character, including the disreputable Claudio Conde whose release from jail in Valencia Lope later obtained. There is some evidence that Isabel may also have gone to Lisbon to see him off; if she went, her presence did not stop Lope from intimacy with a Lisbon prostitute. Some years later he wrote the Duke of Sessa that when he offered to pay the mother some *escudos* for his night with her daughter, the daughter refused to let her accept, saying "No me pago cuando me huelgo." [5]

Before the thirty thousand-man Armada embarked, the Church

gave them confession, holy communion, and a Bull of Indulgence which absolved them of all mortal sins and opened the gates of Paradise to all who might be killed in battle.

During the disastrous expedition in which his brother Juan was killed, Lope is said to have composed a long epic poem entitled *The Beauty of Angelica* (*La hermosura de Angélica*) in imitation of Ariosto. After the defeat of the Armada, it is thought that Lope's galleon, the "San Juan," touched off Ireland, then sailed to Coruña. Since Lope was still under banishment from Madrid, Isabel met him in Toledo, and they traveled with his bosom friend, Claudio Conde, and Gaspar de Porres, the impresario, to Valencia to take up residence. Lope learned some of the Valencian dialect and soon was inserting Valencian songs into his plays and humorous Valencian phrases into the mouths of his *graciosos*. He utilized Valencian lore in *The College Half-wit* (*El bobo del Colegio*), *The Beach of Valencia* (*El grao de Valencia*), *The Valencian Lunatics* (*Los locos de Valencia*), and *The Flowers of Don Juan* (*Las flores de don Juan*). In Valencia he witnessed the first showing of numerous of his plays and began in feverish earnest his career as a professional playwright. Valencia received him cordially, rewarded him generously, and proffered her own playwrights as his disciples.

Evidence points to a Lope able to keep his polygynous spirit in check during his marriage to Isabel. They resided in Valencia from 1588 until 1590, then moved to Toledo where he entered the service of the Marqués de Malpica for a few months. The same year, 1590, Lope joined the staff of the Duke of Alba de Tormes, in the province of Salamanca, remaining with him several years. Around 1594 catastrophe struck Lope's family.

Isabel died giving birth to a little girl, named Teodora, after the Saint, and the child survived her mother only a few months. Lope yearned to leave the scene of his sorrow. He poured out his grief, in art by writing verse and in deed by arranging to sell at auction all the household reminders of the double death of wife and child. A document survives giving details of the items sold, listing hats, slippers, a black velvet sleeve adorned with gold and glass beads, a fan, a red dress, "three tiny blouses for a little girl." One of his sonnets addressed to little Teodora begins:

My beloved, born out of my sorrows,
Celestial likeness of my Belisa, who
with gentle speech and sweet laughter
matched exile with consolation . . .

ANTONIA TRILLO DE ARMENTA, *1596(?)*. Lope, being Lope, did not long retread the past nor keep sex at arm's length. His sentence to exile having been canceled in 1595, he returned to his beloved Madrid where he quickly made an abrupt transition from gravity to gaiety—and back again. Toward the spring of 1595 Antonia Trillo de Armenta, the widow of Luis Puig (or Puche), a woman well off, of easy virtue, in her thirties, turned Lope's melancholy mood so quickly into gaiety that one has to conclude that his moods shifted easily.

Lope's friendship with Antonia developed *allegro con brio*. She was a lady much gossiped about, or "de mucha historia," as they say in Spanish, although a sister, Catalina, had taken the veil. Since Antonia's parents and husband were dead, she was a free woman, as wives with living husbands, and daughters, never were. Information about her ends here, except for one more document, from police files, dated 1596, charging Lope with cohabitating with her. Scandalmongering pressed in upon Lope who soon returned to Alba de Tormes; there the Duke of Alba dismissed him for good. Some time later Antonia Trillo de Armenta became Antonia Trillo de Moreno, by marriage to a servant of His Majesty Felipe II, Pablo Moreno, whom she survived. She probably passed out of Lope's life for good in 1596, and certainly out of this world in 1631, preceding Lope by four years.

MICAELA DE LUJÁN (LUCINDA) *1598(?)–1607(?)*. The sixteenth century was drawing to a close when chance brought Lope into a relationship that proved to be productive of children as well as of literature: he met Diego Díaz de Castro's wife, Micaela de Luján, blue-eyed, beautiful, blonde, gay, illiterate, and prolific.[6] She probably had two children already by Díaz—Agustina and Dionisia. Soon she began to cohabit with Lope, and until her husband died in 1603, it was anybody's guess who fathered the remaining six children, Mariana, Angela, Lope Félix, Jacinta, Marcela, and Juan. The chances heavily favor Lope's paternity, for Diego Díaz traveled with barnstorming actors, perhaps as far away as Peru.[7] Lope recorded his first meeting with Micaela de Luján religiously—literally so; instead of noting down a prosaic numerical calendar date, he dated their meeting, in a sonnet, as the eve of the Day of the Assumption, August 14:

> It was on the joyous eve of the day the
> peerless earth-born (Mary) left her
> mortal coil and our warring humanity
> for Heaven . . . when Love first showed
> me Lucinda's beautiful glance, which
> consumed me like lightning . . .

Intimacy arrived slowly. Micaela held her emotions in check and procrastinated so exasperatingly that she provoked the infatuated poet into expressing his impatience in terms of a Leah-Rachel sonnet beginning, "Jacob served seven long years . . ."

JUANA DE GUARDO, *1598–1613.* The Leah in the sonnet above is Juana de Guardo, whom Lope married in 1598. She was the plain daughter of a wealthy Madrid butcher-fishmonger whom Lope expected, in vain, to put him on easy street. She partly manacled his intimacy with Micaela, his "Rachel," so that Lope regretted the marriage keenly and wished unequivocally, in verse, that she would soon join her Maker. Although a woman of delicate health, she survived his imprecations and his Lotharian conduct, as well as the bearing of four children, until 1613. Lope never gave her a poetic name as he had given his first wife, Isabel de Urbina; by contrast he gave Micaela de Luján two: "Lucinda," and "Camila Lucinda," using the first most frequently. In 1602 in an epic poem entitled *The Beauty of Angélica* (*La hermosura de Angélica*), trembling with passion, he placed "Lucinda" (Micaela) in Canto V, proclaiming she would have won any beauty contest against the imaginary Angélica if she had lived in her day. The Angélica volume contained a poem signed "Lucinda," who, as we noted above, was illiterate. The poem is laudatory of Lope—or one should say self-laudatory. Lope and "Lucinda" lived together in Seville, Granada, and Madrid. When children came, they unabashedly assigned their paternity to her husband, until his death in 1603, after which they baptized them as orphans, "parents unknown" ("de padres desconocidos.")

Toward the middle of 1604 Lope and Juana left Seville for Toledo. Toledo was not a large city, but he set up two households there, near each other, one for his love without marriage (Micaela de Luján), and the other for his marriage without love (Juana de Guardo). He maintained two households for some years. In a letter dated August 4, 1604, addressed to a doctor friend of his, he left an unequivocal description of his life in this equivocal situation. In part he said, "My health is fine . . . Doña Juana is about to have a baby, which certainly doesn't lighten my job any . . . Toledo is expensive, but wonderful . . . If people there [in Madrid] are talking speculatively about my plays and claiming I write them for fame, set them straight and say *I write for money*." It is the chatty letter of a man apparently just going about his daily affairs with business more or less as usual.

Early in May of 1605 Micaela gave birth to a daughter, Marcela, who was to become a nun early in life and bring solace to Lope on numerous needful occasions. She was to become a kind of compensation for Lopito, her delinquent older brother, who caused his father much paternal anguish.

Lope's dual household in Toledo did not diminish the esteem shown him by the city-hall authorities. Soon after Marcela's birth, "de padres desconocidos," a son was born to the King, and Toledo employed Lope to organize a poetry contest in celebration of the royal birth. The royal son was Prince Felipe, later King Felipe IV. Lope was assigned the task "as an experienced Toledo poet whom everybody knows because he has resided in Toledo and regarded it as his mother . . ." For the Toledo celebration he acted as judge of the poetry contest and contributed verse of his own. He badly exploits his position as judge by contributing a "Sonnet by Lucinda Serrana," under the pet name of his illiterate Micaela. Apparently this sort of deceit annoyed no one, for the royal birthday celebration was happily festive and the attendance was large. It included several famous contemporaries of Lope's and numerous friends. His wife stayed away.

JERÓNIMA DE BURGOS (LA SEÑORA GERARDA), *1613*. By 1607 Lope had reduced his two Toledo households to one, for Micaela de Luján had gone to live in Madrid where she gave birth on January 28 to a son named Lope Félix junior. Michaela seemed to have erred in the choice of one of the godparents, a beautiful and talented married actress named Jerónima de Burgos. Jerónima had been, from all indications, a friend of Micaela's. However, the meager information available intimates that friend Jerónima replaced Micaela in Lope's affections. Jerónima de Burgos crashed at this time into Lope's life and thus into Spanish poetry.

There is some evidence that Micaela continued to live in Madrid with her children until around 1613, the year Juana de Guardo died leaving Lope a widower for the second time. Micaela probably left her children, Marcela and Lopito, to live with him on Francos (today Cervantes) Street, in the house preserved today as *la casa de Lope de Vega*. On Micaela's tomb Lope wrote one of his most enigmatically complimentary sonnets, entitled "On the Death of a Singular Actress," which concludes as follows:

> She acted every role so convincingly that even
> when she was dying
> her death throes were believed pretended.
> Because she had counterfeited life, everyone
> imagined that she likewise
> was counterfeiting death . . .

Illiterate, beautiful "Camila Lucinda" (Micaela de Luján) moved mysteriously in and out of Lope's poetry repeatedly, wrapped in a certain imprecision which reflected often only the shadow in her Visigothic blue eyes and her golden hair, uncommon in Castile.

Around 1599, during the time of the Micaela de Luján liaison, Lope had a son, Fernando Pellicer, who became Fray Vicente. His mother was an unidentified woman in Valencia; Lope hinted in verse at a simultaneous affair in 1602 with another unidentified woman whom he called Flora. Nothing further is known of either.

Lope gave Jerónima de Burgos the pet name of "la señora Gerarda" in his letters to the Duke of Sessa. Born around 1580, she was the daughter of a pastry cook from Valladolid, who turned her over when she was a teen-ager to a company of strolling players for whom she sang and danced. In her twenties she married an actor, Pedro de Valdés. Possessed of great charm, wit, and beauty, she became famous as an actress, especially in the Corpus Christi plays in Toledo and Seville, and she inspired Lope to write the sprightly comedy *Miss Simpleton* (*La dama boba*) and other plays suited to her particular talents. Jerónima was "fast" in the peculiarly reverse sense of that word, meaning yielding, numbering several men among her lovers, probably including Lope's patron, the Duke of Sessa. She had a passion for money, jewels, clothes, and for Lope for whom she would do anything, even give him money earned by selling herself. They were living together in 1614 when Lope became a priest, and Sáinz de Robles recreates imaginatively the scene of Lope and his mistress closeted in his praying room the first time he wore the cloth:

"Lope had shaved off his mustache, by order of the Bishop. . . . With his razor in his right hand, standing angrily before the mirror, talking a blue streak, he moved back, and Gerarda (i. e., Jerónima) observed him attentively. Frocked! Next head and face shaven clean! He looked like some other guy! The anger of the one and the surprise of the other curdled into an exchange of glances; from their glances arose laughter, from their laughter, kisses . . . seemingly not like renovated kisses, but brand new ones. Thus the first congratulations received by Lope, the priest." [8] It might have happened this way.

But when Jerónima went from plump to obese and began to drink excessively, Lope left her. In a letter to the Duke of Sessa, he called her "Miss Fatty" and unsympathetically mocked her chronic alcoholism. Once she donned nun's clothes, perhaps just to express her desire to abandon theatrical circles with their sinful atmosphere, and when Lope heard about it, he ridiculed her, saying he wondered just what a scapulary would look like dangling above her big pot-belly (*panza*). His unkindest cuts at Jerónima were theologically contrived: "On Judgment Day they say people will return thirty-three years old. I hope to God you and I return with this age . . . so that at least we can remember who we were . . ."

Here Lope, as always, alternately attracts and repels. He hoped by taking the cloth to reform once and for all, to become a new man. But he did not; indeed, could not. For him the continued order of the day, even after being frocked, was "pecar, hacer penitencia y vuelta a pecar" (sin, repent, then sin again).

LUCÍA DE SALCEDO (LA LOCA), *1616.* Lope's next known mistress was to be Lucía de Salcedo, "la loca." In the heat of a Castilian July, Lope left Madrid for Avila on muleback to request a chaplaincy from his old friend and patron, Jerónimo Manrique, in the Church of Saint Segundo in Ávila. The position paid 150 ducats annually. He obtained the job, and on the return trip via Segovia went fishing with a producer named Sánchez, finished a play, and renewed his intimacies with Lucía de Salcedo, the merry widow of a deceased actor named Jerónimo de Hugarte.

Lucía de Salcedo's name appears among the lists of actresses of the then widely known theatrical companies of Antonia de Riquelme and Hernán Sánchez de Vargas. Her notoriety was such that she probably was the model for a description of an actress written by a contemporary novelist, Salas Barbadillo, in *The House of Chaste Pleasure (Casa del placer honesto):* "She was a woman of beautiful and genteel disposition, golden hair . . . eyes so blue they were a rebuff to sapphires, rivals of the heavens; a mouth rather large than small . . . , teeth so beautiful it was a pity to keep them condemned to confinement; a complexion free of make-up . . . and in judgment, a fickle featherbrain."

Lope wrote of Lucía de Salcedo as "la loca." They lived together for a while in Madrid, before 1616, where she also acted in his plays. Later she joined a traveling company subsidized by a nobleman. Lope wrote Sessa of her travels, of his distress on failing to receive her letters for days; of his rush trip to Valencia, June 20, 1616, ostensibly to visit his bastard son, Fray Vicente, but in reality to be with her; of his grave illness in Valencia and of her visits to his bedside; of his willingness to share her with Sessa; of his return in the middle of August to Madrid; of the ungracious conclusion of the whole affair. "Now I want only," said Lope in a letter to Sessa, "to see that stupid love affair hanged in the plaza for everyone to see, like those criminals who have a sign pinned on them by edict which says: *Hanged for Infamy.*"

He complained that she returned him deception for "sincerity and truth," this Lope who on another occasion had declared unequivocally, "In love, lying and telling the truth are one and the same thing."

Behind an aging, arrogant Lope stands a string of feminine images, some misty and unclear, some all too clear in a number of aspects. All of them come from the *pueblo* (the common people), none from the aristocracy, as was the case with Goya in the succeeding century. These women of the people, by their common plebeianism, give us some insight into the eroticism of Lope de Vega: actress Elena Osorio, sensuous, ardent, violent, unforgettable, unfaithful, childless; first wife Isabel de Urbina, for Lope a Don Juanesque caprice that left in his soul a feeling of regret for the faithful love he could not reciprocate; the actor's wife, Micaela de Luján, hers a gentle but intense, domestic, generative love without violent eruption, giving him what Juana de Guardo never could; the widow of easy virtue Antonia Trillo de Armenta; the witty, unhappily married and promiscuous actress Jerónima de Burgos; the beautiful, fickle, featherbrained actress, Lucía de Salcedo; the unidentified mistresses who gave him two sons, both destined for the cloth. Why were none of his womenfolk from the aristocracy? One can only guess the answer. Most, possibly all, remained on the frontier of the amative domain of Lope, a long way from the center.[9] The woman who reached his heart of hearts arrived in his life late, not until 1616, when Lope was six years beyond the half-century mark.

MARTA DE NEVARES (AMARILIS), *1617(?)–1632.* This woman, the ideal he had searched for, was Marta de Nevares, or "Amarilis." I call on Anthony Trollope, in *Barchester Towers* (Chapter 37) to banish the idea that perhaps Amarilis, too, was kept at the frontier of Lope's eroticism because he was aging:

It is, we believe, common with young men of five and twenty to look on their seniors—on men of, say, double their own age—as so many stocks and stones—stocks and stones, that is, in regard to feminine beauty. There never was a greater mistake. Women, indeed, generally know better; but on this subject men of one age are thoroughly ignorant of what is the very nature of mankind of other ages. No experience of what goes on in the world, no reading of history, no observation of life, has any effect in teaching the truth. Men of fifty don't dance mazurkas, being generally too fat and wheezy; nor do they sit for the hour together on river banks at their mistresses' feet, being somewhat afraid of rheumatism. But for real true love, love at first sight, love to devotion, love that robs a man of his sleep, love that "will gaze an eagle blind," love that "will hear the lowest sound when the suspicious tread of theft is stopped," love that is "like a Hercules, still climbing trees in the Hesperides,"—we believe the best age is from forty-five to seventy; up to that, men are generally given to mere flirting.

When Lope met "Amarilis," his brief affair with the giddy Lucía de Salcedo was drawing to a close. Having become the most celebrated dramatist in Spain, he was living in a goldfish bowl. Lucía, out of spite, was denouncing him to all who would listen. Marta de Nevares ("Amarilis"), Lucía's antithesis, inspired love and religion; in an early letter about her, Lope wrote Sessa that he "loved her like a nun." Her nunnishness seemed to heighten the ecstasy of their intimacy. She was in her middle twenties, Lope his middle fifties. He was flattered by the attentions of so young and beautiful a woman, and she in turn by his fame. With adoration he spoke of her in medico-religious-sexual terms. He left letters and poetry which idolize her. "At last I've found the physician for my wounds . . . ," he wrote to the Duke of Sessa. What a physician! Green eyes, eyelashes black as night, naturally curly hair, rosy complexion, "shapely, slender legs, which she knows how to pose teasingly," nice hands, talent for accompanying him in playing a musical instrument, skill in dancing, genius for writing verse "better than Sappho." And as for singing, ". . . her heavenly voice has an angelical quality which leads one to high and noble meditation." He was indeed a theologian in love.

But being a priest was only a part of his equivocal situation. Marta had a husband. She had been forced to marry at age thirteen, to her eternal sorrow, a man named Roque Hernández. He was, according to a very prejudiced, ungracious Lope, "of a churlish mind," all business, insensitive; besides "the hair on his body began at his eyes and ended at his toes." A worse mis-marriage could hardly have been made for a sensitive young girl. Meeting Lope, who lived not far away, brought her im-measurable, though illicit, joy and satisfaction. He was the an-tithesis of her husband.

Months passed, Roque Hernández' sullen distrust of Marta caused him to resort to threats of violence if she did not stop seeing Lope. One can follow in detail the story of Hernández' increasing resentment as described by Lope in his letters to Sessa. This Hernández, incidentally, is the scribe who copied Lope's plays for the Duke of Sessa, by now obsessed with a mania for collecting everything Lope wrote, including his love letters. Towards the end of July of 1617, when Marta was ex-pecting Lope's child, he wrote again to Sessa, "I went to Ama-rilis' home. She fed me and said, 'If I weren't in this condition [pregnant], there would be bulls [virility] here the same as in the bullring." In this letter and others Lope ridiculed Hernández in such a way that we are able to glimpse indirectly into the mind of Marta. Lope's letters clearly indicate that Marta, fully as much as Lope, ridiculed her husband and hoped to be free of his shackles.

After a painful and prolonged delivery, the child was born, and Lope and Marta had her baptized Antonia Clara, the legiti-mate daughter of Marta and Roque Hernández, knowing other-wise. A fiesta for the Mass of Purification of Marta was held a few days later in Atocha, Lope playing openly the role everyone knew was illegally his.

By the end of 1617 Roque Hernández' fury had got beyond control. Following an attempt to murder Lope in a street in Madrid, Lope wrote Sessa that he was certain the instigator was Hernández. Then, to the first relatively stable relationship of Lope's life, came a series of mishaps. Marta, pregnant again, had a miscarriage. Lope became quite ill, and after recovery, had to have a tooth pulled. Marta began her bitter litigation for *divorcio* (separation, not divorce) from her husband. The suit, of course, in an ecclesiastical court, dragged out over many months and caused many oppressive hours for Lope and his mistress. Marta finally obtained a separation decree, but the husband appealed leaving the lovers in a continual purgatory of suspense. Then in the midst of everything Roque Hernández died. At this turn of events Lope expressed a savage joy in his correspondence. He wrote not a word of pity. Quite the contrary. In the dedication to Marta of a bawdy comedy entitled *The Valencian Widow* (*La viuda valenciana*), Lope continued to mock and ridicule Roque Hernández and hinted (to say the least) at having bribed the husband's physician to murder him. "Bully for Death, she's all right! What medicine couldn't remedy, death finished off in five days with an ill-timed purgative, two accelerated bleedings, and a doctor with greater zeal for your [Marta's] freedom than the life of your husband . . . so strong was the wish that he be off . . ."

Very likely some time passed after Hernández' death before Marta went with her little daughter, Antonia Clara, to live with Lope, who by now had quite a heterogeneous, and perhaps sometimes discordant, household. Of the fruits of his love affairs and his two marriages all were now gone except three children: Lope Félix (Lopito), child of his inamorata Micaela de Luján; Feliciana, daughter of his second wife, Juana; and Antonia Clara, still an infant, with her mother, Marta. Surely, even in morally lax seventeenth-century Madrid, this priest's household must have caused constant eyebrow lifting and ceaseless talk.

Lope, as usual in need of money, sought the position of His Majesty's Royal Chronicler. While waiting for a reply to his petition—it always resulted in "waiting" at its most formidable to ask Felipe IV's functionaries for anything—he busied himself with, in his own words, "saying masses, praying, Holy Week activities" and other priestly duties. And with being a *bon père de famille*. But he waited in vain, for the position went to a rival. Lope's private life was probably a determining factor in his failure.

Sometime in the middle 1620's multiple catastrophes began to strike Lope's household. Marta gradually lost her sight from causes unknown, although she assumed that witchcraft was back of it all. To seek a cure, she and Lope went on a novena to Santa Lucía. Toward the end of the winter of 1628 Lope wrote, "surely the angels of God will plead with Him for such beautiful eyes." But perhaps they didn't, for the novena was fruitless. They consulted an English woman who applied pain-causing plasters. In vain. Next they went on a week's pilgrimage. Feliciana, Marcela, and Marta's sister accompanied them "dressed as farm girls," to the Monastery of Our Lady of the Cross, where they prayed to Saint Joan. Again in vain. Marta went totally blind. Lope cared for her tenderly, solicitously, and wrote a great deal of verse expressing his sorrow and hers. As always, for him, to live was to create. He turned this tragic part of his life into poetry, using, as customary, pastoral names and pastoral settings. He identified himself completely with his beloved, calling her blindness, her pain, her fear of hell, all his own.

> Beloved eyes, if I saw the light of
> heaven through you, how now can I see
> anything without you?
> (Ojos, si vi por vos la luz del cielo,
> ¿Qué cosa veré ya sin vuestra vista?)
> —Eclogue to "Amarilis"

Alonso Zamora Vicente[10] highlights Marta's strong influence on Lope's literary production. She entered his life late, rejuvenated him. His thoughts were constantly about her. And as he was wont to do, he continued to translate his daily life and thought into poetry, even including such extreme emotion as the ruthless joy he expressed in his dedication of *The Valencian Widow* (*La viuda valenciana*) to Marta.

The following year (1621) he dedicated *Women Without Men* (*Las mujeres sin hombres*) to Marta, as well as a novel entitled *The Fortunes of Diana* (*Las fortunas de Diana*). From certain statements in his dedication, one deduces that she had suggested he write short stories "like Cervantes"; this is clear evidence that he talked over literary projects with her. Lope dedicated several works to Marta, analyzed her beauty, transposed it into sonnets, frequently translated their intimacies into verse. He burst anew with energy and his production rate soared during the first of these golden—though sometimes blighted—years with Marta.

Lope's last years brought increasing fame, but they also brought him continuing chastising disasters. All his disasters seemed to him God's fitting, if frightful, castigation for sin.

Lopito, the unruly son, continued to be incorrigible. Amarilis lost her sanity, at times becoming so violent she tore off her clothes. Her sanity finally returned, but soon after the beginning of 1632 she died, leaving Lope in a state of savage melancholy and so infinitely tired and discouraged that he asked Sessa to make him his personal chaplain so that he might discontinue writing for the stage and finish his weary days with at least a meager measure of tranquility. "Your Excellency," he wrote Sessa, "for days now I have wanted to stop writing for the stage, because of old age and fatigue and affliction of the spirit. . . . With the failure of two plays, well written but indifferently received, I have come to realize that either people now want plays written by younger men, or heaven frowns upon the idea of death catching a priest in the act of creating mediocre comedies; so I propose to stop playwriting entirely in order to avoid being like beautiful women who become merely the butt of ridicule in their old age; I beg your Excellency to give a job openly to one who has been your servant secretly for twenty-five years; without your help I'm at the end of my tether; you could give me a moderate salary to supplement the pension I already have and help me through the brief time remaining for me on this earth. The office of Chaplain would be appropriate. I would say mass for your Excellency daily and [as your secretary] write whatever you wished. . . ." Sessa refused.

On a pearl-hunting expedition off the coast of the Island of Margarita in 1634, Lopito drowned.

The same year brought the worst paternal heartbreak of all. Cristóbal Tenorio, a Madrid hidalgo, abducted Lope's beloved daughter-stenographer-companion, Antonia Clara, and it is believed that Lope never saw her again.

After Feliciana's marriage around 1633, Antonia Clara's abduction, and Lopito's death, Lope found his home on Francos Street peopled only by memories and ghosts from the past. Loneliness and misery became sonnets and pastoral poems and religious literature, and, to relieve the tedium of sadness, he turned to writing a cat-lover's burlesque poem called *The Battle of Cats* (*La gatomaquia*).

Now in his seventies, Lope repented daily for his misdeeds:

as he approached the end, his theological frame of reference made any other course unlikely. He scourged himself every Friday, carried out the office of priest, and looked across the roof tops, as one may still do today, at the convent where his beloved Marcela had long since been cloistered, barefoot. Feliciana, his only legitimate child to reach adulthood, had two children—a daughter who took the veil, and a son, Captain Luis Antonio de Usátegui y Vega, who joined His Majesty's armed forces and perished in Milan. So Lope, father of fourteen (or more) children by ten (or more) women, suffered the extinction of his line.[11] Only his works, and they only in part, survived him.

In spite of the bewitchment of sex to Lope de Vega, its lures remained like shackles to his theological mind, shackles which he attempted daily to throw off, fetters to be broken—always, however, in vain. His life is vividly summarized in the poignant phrase quoted above: "Pecar, hacer penitencia y vuelta a pecar" ("Sin, repent, and then sin again"). Two of his own sonnets epitomize aptly the two hostile elements in the makeup of his sin-conscious character: "A Gloss on Love," and "A Gloss on Repentance."

### A Gloss on Love

FLOUNDERING, venturing, becoming angry,
gruff, tender, receptive, aloof,
spirited, listless, lifeless, lively,
loyal, treacherous, cowardly, brave;
never finding purpose or tranquility
except in the beloved;
seeming joyous, sad, humble, arrogant,
furious, courageous, fugitive,
smug, irritable, suspicious;
ignoring clear disillusionment,
drinking down poison like a mild rum,
disregarding advantage, courting danger;
believing that heaven is possible in hell,
bartering body and soul for a dream;
LOVE IS ALL THESE. WHOEVER TASTED IT KNOWS.

—Lope de Vega
(Translated by the author)

## The Man Lope de Vega

### A Gloss on Repentance

Lord, what am I, that, with unceasing care,
    Thou didst seek after me, that thou didst wait,
    Wet with unhealthy dews, before my gate,
    And pass the gloomy nights of winter there?
Oh, strange delusion, that I did not greet
    Thy blest approach! and oh, to Heaven how lost,
    If my ingratitude's unkindly frost
    Has chilled the bleeding wounds upon thy feet!
How oft my guardian angel gently cried,
    "Soul, from thy casement look, and thou shalt see
    How he persists to knock and wait for thee!"
And, oh! how often to that voice of sorrow,
    "Tomorrow we will open," I replied,
    And when the morrow came I answered still,
    "Tomorrow."

—Translated by Longfellow

# CHAPTER 2

## *Spanish Drama in Lope's Time*

### I  *The Physical Stage*

FROM EMPTY LOT TO THEATER—DOÑA PACHECA'S YARD.[1]  When
Lope de Vega was a child, Spanish drama was in a sense also
a child—one might say an old child, for it was old in years and,
although willingly experimental from 1492 on, it remained generally childlike, artless, ingenuous, with occasional accompanying attractive primitive-lyrical characteristics, as for example in
Gil Vicente's playlets. It may be classified roughly into: *religious
drama* performed on church holidays in the town squares on carts
with all the pomp and circumstance that available funds and
enthusiasm permitted; *closet drama* performed in Latin at the
universities; and *barnstorming theater* performed by traveling
players, such as Lope de Rueda (d. 1565). The major physical
element lacking, of course, was permanent housing. Spanish
cities, including even Madrid, the new capital from 1561 on of
a vast world empire, lacked permanent "legitimate" playhouses.
Lope was born into this situation and was destined to see several
giant steps forward toward permanent theaters.

Lope de Vega was only a boy when certain religious brotherhoods (*cofradías*) of Madrid began to sublet *corrales* (open court
yards, or vacant lots) in the city to players in order to share
their profits and further their own charitable work, caring for
the indigent old and sick.[2] For a number of years nearly all the
performances in Madrid took place in these open courts. Then
the brotherhoods, alert to the possibilities of sources of much-
needed income, began to purchase their own lots and construct
their own permanent open-air theaters. The Corral de la Cruz
(Corral of the Cross) was the first one, in 1579. The Corral del
Príncipe followed not long afterwards (1582), and there were
soon others. The public was so eager to attend the Cruz on its
opening afternoon that they crowded in even before construction

work was completed. Other *corrales* soon made their appearance, but the Cruz and the Príncipe were the most enduring. The latter, originally known as la Pacheca, from the name of its owner, Isabel Pacheco, eventually became the Teatro Español and stands to this day in the same original location. It may be the oldest theater in the Western Hemisphere still in operation. It remained an open-air theater until 1745, the Cruz until 1743. The Cruz and the Príncipe were the scene of premières or "opening afternoons"—there were no downtown evening shows—of the best works of Spain's drama of the *Siglo de oro*.

Seville, Toledo, Valencia, Granada, Córdoba, Barcelona, Valladolid and other cities soon had thriving *corrales* christened with such names as Toledo's El mesón de la Fruta, (Fruit Inn), La Cárcel Vieja (Ye Olde Jail), Don Juan, and Doña Elvira (Seville's most famous), affording Lope a market for his wares early in his lifetime. By the end of the sixteenth century most of Spain's large cities had constructed resident theaters for the vast deluge of plays soon to follow.

But show business encountered drawbacks and handicaps. Not until the end of the 1580's did the civil government permit the *corrales* to open except on holidays and Sundays. Then, a few years later, Tuesdays and Thursdays and other religious holidays became theater days too; for example, fifteen days before Shrovetide.

From October until April the shows began at 2:00 P.M.; in the spring at 3:00 P.M.; in summer at 4:00. The doors were opened at noon. The demand for seats was so brisk and steady that one had to come early or send a servant to hold a place. Hawkers sold candy, fruits, pastry, wine, and water, using snow brought down from the sierra to cool them. For advertising the management sent out street criers and plastered the walls of busy street corners with large, gaudy, hand-made posters which gave the title of the play and the names of the principal actors but often omitted the name of the author.

Theatergoers paid admission at the entrance. Once inside, they paid again for a place to sit or else they stood with the generally rowdy *mosqueteros* (standees)—the terror of actors, easily bored, or riled, or both at once, and prone to throw ripe vegetables and fruits when displeased. Overhead was a stretched-out canvas principally to protect from the sun, rarely from rain which is usually light and quick during summer in Madrid. One might sit on the sides in the *gradas* (graduated seats), on the portable benches in front of the stage in rows that reached almost to the rear, or look out from a window of a room (*aposento*) on either side, the most costly seats of all, often rented for an entire season by the wealthy, sometimes passed down from father to son.

Women were not only segregated, but obliged to enter by a separate door to a rear balcony, called the *cazuela* (stewpot). If a man let his emotions cloud his judgment and entered the women's balcony, the police would seize him and penalize him, sometimes with exile for a space of time from Madrid. The *mosqueteros* as well as the *caballeros* flirted with the pretty women in the balcony, with lots of incitement from the women, according to contemporary reports. There was orchestra music. Once the show began, there was no let-up for the actors and little for the musicians. Before Act I came a song and a dance, perhaps a belly dance called *la chacona:* "That CHACONA is a treasure—/ makes life a real pleasure."

Next a comedian recited a *loa* (burlesque skit). Then between Acts I and II a pretty actress danced, again probably a showstopper such as the sexy *zarabanda* (saraband). Between Acts II and III the company performed an *entremés* (farce in verse), or a mask. Nobody got a *descanso* (intermission). When the play was over—one may not say "when the curtain went down," for there was no front curtain—an actor stepped forward to beg the *ilustre senado* (illustrious audience) for applause and pardon for mistakes. All spectators were forthwith cleared out. The law required an empty *corral* one hour before sundown.

In spite of their exhausting work, actors were poorly paid. A then-famous actress named Amarilis received only two hundred reals per performance. Impresarios paid authors in the neighborhood of one hundred reals for a *loa,* three hundred for an *entremés* or a *mojiganga* (mask), from two hundred to four hundred for a *sainete* (one-act farce in verse), from four hundred to five hundred for a three-act play. But to Lope, a magnet for big crowds, they paid as high as eight hundred or even one thousand reals.

[ 44 ]

The theater had numerous civil and ecclesiastical enemies who periodically called it a wicked hag, the ally of Satan. These enemies hurt it grievously but never permanently, repressed it for a while but never silenced it. If the theater had powerful enemies, it had more powerful friends. When its enemies were in the saddle, they could create lean times for hundreds who derived their livelihood from it. Saving money against rainy days would have required austere living, a not very likely practice among bohemians of any century. Once, at the end of the 16th century (1597), Felipe II closed the theaters because of a death in the royal family. Certain clergy took advantage of the occasion and attempted to make the closure permanent. Felipe was persuaded by his confessor to at least consider it. He referred the matter to three theologians who deliberated for five months and then decided on closure. Felipe issued a royal proclamation: No more plays in Madrid. The year was 1598 and Lope was thirty-six. The closing was a severe financial blow to him as to all other theater people.

Among other arguments offered by the three churchmen for their drastic action, they said that the theater makes Spaniards soft and womanish and unfits them for war. But Felipe's decree did not stand for long. The brotherhoods, supporting poorhouses and several other charitable organizations, roused to battle fury and caused a furor: closed shows meant closed asylums for the poor and rejected. On April 17, 1599, the new King, Felipe III, overruled his confessor, a powerful anti-theater theologian, and the shows were open for business again. There were stricter rules than before—but rules soon broken—for the new King was a bored monarch and sought entertainment, and most Spaniards loved their legitimate theater too much. The new regulations said no more belly dancing, no more sexy songs, no more women on the stage; only four companies to be licensed in all Madrid; no more admission of priests into the theater, or friars, or other men of the cloth; no more licensing of any play until it had first been witnessed by upstanding citizens (*personas graves*); no more weekday playgoing, performances to be reserved for Sundays and certain movable feast days. But soon the old cynical Spanish phrase about commands from officials began to be applied: "Se obedece, pero no se cumple" (We obey the rule but do not enforce it). And so on until the next temporary closure, followed again by reopening.

Of course, reform moods shift quickly. They hit Madrid in 1598, and 1600, and struck again in 1603, 1608, 1613, and 1615. Yet just then, in spite of these deterrents, Spanish drama showed a great burst of energy, for the time, the place, and the man had coincided: the time, the Golden Age of Spanish political power and culture; the place, Madrid, capital of world empire, magnet of the world's gold and its people; the man, Lope de Vega, "the prodigy of nature" ("el monstruo de la naturaleza"), the creator of the national Spanish drama, the most prolific playwright of all time.

BEGUILE WITH CREAKY ILLUSION—SOME TRICKS OF THE TRADE. The secular stage available to Lope, especially after 1600, was ingenious if creaky. It had quite a variety of machinery but no front curtain. Curtains hung along the sides and rear. Every *corral* had a recessed area, a *nicho,* generally in the middle of the back-stage and concealed by a curtain; a raised portion, a sort of gallery, running across the back and sturdy enough to support both people and horses; trap doors opening at various points into the sub-stage compartments; two doors at the back, one on each side; a common dressing room for both sexes; machine devices of a relatively crude nature. No record of the precise dimensions of the usual secular stage has survived. It was probably not so deep as in a modern theater, but rather wide, and projected out into the theater.

Machine devices (*tramoyas*) were common and included pulleys for lifting, paper and cloth-covered frames simulating clouds, suns, moons, and stars—especially for religious dramas of which Lope wrote a large number. Actual scenery was simple and the furnishings employed were inexpensive in the *corrales.* The big money was spent at the Palace theaters, particularly during the reign of Felipe IV (1621–65), where productions were spectacular and costly, often with a grandiose Cecil De Mille touch. During this era, not only royalty but the wealthy nobility also spent lavishly to subsidize their own theaters.

Directors made consistent use of small curtain disclosures which revealed previously prepared scenes in the *nicho.* The curtain was pulled open at the proper moment, a contrivance found very early on the Spanish stage. Often there were two parallel niches, one on stage level, the other on the rear raised platform, for simultaneous disclosure. Sometimes a double curtain was placed in the same niche, one in front pulled first, then the second one behind. These multiple curtains widened the scope of the stage and yet were inexpensively constructed. Construction of sets was often specified by the producer in detail. Niche curtains are the forerunners of the modern front curtains. They constituted a technical implement which allowed dramatists some measure of creative freedom. Drums, music, and off-stage noises were used to focus attention on them, and disclosure scenes often became high spots in the play. Lope repeatedly used disclosures showing executions, torture, massed effects of horror, and blood and violence. It all might be classified under the heading of the use of the grotesque for startling the audience. There is need for more research on Lope's utilization of stage machinery. His contemporary, playwright Andrés de Claramonte, complained enviously that Lope depended on *caballos y carpinteros* ("horses and carpenters") to make his plays come off.

The chief source for knowledge of stage devices in Lope's day is found in stage directions written in the plays themselves. I summarize below a few of the props called for within the plays by the authors. I purposely chose rather spectacular examples from hundreds collected by William Rowe Weaver.[3] Many were, of course, unspectacular.

Books might explode, devils disappear in flames, cats scurry across the stage with firecrackers tied to their tails, men be shown burning in hell, people riding a horse or donkey. Some of the single-curtain disclosures in the niches were genuine showstoppers; a woman holding the severed head of a man in her hands, a man crucified wearing a crown of thorns (Lope de Vega, *The Outrageous Saint, La fianza satisfecha*, Act III), the Pope blessing France and Spain while they embrace each other (Lope de Vega, *Charles V in France, Carlos V en Francia*, Act III), a peasant throwing rocks on a government official from above, etc.

Stage machinery was used repeatedly to highlight the unusual or even sensational: women hanging by their hair; a saint transported by the hair of the head at jet speed from Asia to Europe; clouds as mobile device for concealment and revelation; *lienzos* and *paños* (canvas drops) representing a panoramic view of a city, the sea, a battle, a tower, or the starry heavens. Wings or flats (*bastidores*) were probably primitive in Lope's time, although the term was used with great frequency in stage directions. Little is known of the chronology of the development of the various devices.

Live animals often appeared on stage—goats, lambs, the *simpatico* little burro, oxen, and, as mentioned above, horses. Men dressed in appropriate skins to represent wild animals. Once a challenge on horseback was acted so realistically that it caused a certain spectator named Ana Muñoz to suffer a miscarriage.

Every kind of food is mentioned. One peculiarly grotesque use of food was in the hideous scene of a vengeful wife, who first tries, in vain, to force her husband to drink his son's blood, then dashes it in his face upon his refusal, while the child's head is suddenly disclosed on the very table before them. Such horror reminds one of some of the excesses of Shakespeare's *Titus Andronicus*. On occasion an ominous gloom was created by the use of black tablecloths, black plates, *aparato todo negro*. Comic touches were also achieved at times by the use of trick pastry filled with soot or flour to discourage a gluttonous monk, or purgative pickles given by a comedian to discomfit and frustrate a rival.

Except for domestic costuming, little or no effort was made to relate costumes to locale. A Turk did not necessarily dress like a Turk. Lope and others made special use of clothing for comic effect: a *gracioso* (like the Mexican clown, Cantinflas) whose trousers were imminently, or actually, falling down; a lady with a grotesque headdress; men and women overdressed in too much finery; funny devils; ghosts in sheets. Of course, directors repeatedly accentuated emphasis on sex by dressing women in men's clothing,[4] a gimmick which Lope highlighted in his *New Art of Play Writing*, or by presenting them in various stages of undress. Characters were made to appear covered with dirt and blood to create the illusion of battle offstage. False noses and pasteboard masks were common. Common props used were ropes, ladders, jewelry, crowns, mirrors, skeletons, heads, coffins, biers, pistols, javelins, daggers, blunderbusses, and everywhere and always swords, as omnipresent as six-shooters in a western.

Dancing and vocal and instrumental music were theater staples. Numerous instruments were played, but the most popular were the guitar, bagpipes (which are still today a familiar sound in Galicia and Asturias), drums, tambourines, and flutes. Dramatic off-stage choral effects were frequent. Approaching storms were suggested in a number of ways, one being Lope's rapidly moving descriptive dialogue, really quite powerfully hypnotic as in *Pretended Truth* (*Lo Fingido Verdadero*). This play is of special interest in studying stage techniques, giving, as it does in detail, the job of each player; and it has a sensational scene in Act I where the Roman Emperor Aurelius is struck down by lightning. The stage directions say: "Simulate thunder and have him [the emperor] fall to the floor as if he had been struck by lightning." Such a scene would require unerring precision on the part of cast and crew.

## II  *Lope's Contemporaries*

In Lope's day Spaniards bolted down play after play with an insatiate hunger; and Spain during most of his lifetime, and for years afterward, teemed with playwrights who gorged, though never appeased, this lusty national appetite for diversion. I give below brief sketches of the most successful of his contemporaries, and at the end of this chapter a list of now nearly forgotten playwrights who strove to achieve eminence but never rose above relative mediocrity.

A prodigious number of plays was produced, some sublime, many excellent, but most merely potboilers. I once compiled an approximate count of both good and mediocre plays produced during Lope's lifetime; the number soared into the thousands.

Sheer quantity itself conveys a message about the exuberant burst of energy, the *furia española,* of the Spanish Golden Age, when one remembers that all plays were composed in verse, hundreds of them interspersed with dancing and music—solo, choral, and orchestral. Such lavishness brought ultimate exhaustion and decline; and even today students of Spanish drama may feel a sort of corollary exhaustion, at times having the sensation of being buried under an avalanche of drama.

Three kings of Spain were contemporary with Lope de Vega: Felipe II (1555–98), Felipe III (1598–1621), and Felipe IV (1621–65). During Felipe II's reign, which approximately coincided with the birth, childhood, and early manhood of Lope, Spanish drama reflected classic, religious, and traditionally Spanish popular currents of thought. These currents converged by the end of the sixteenth century in the drama of Lope, and with him religion and Spanish tradition—from balladry, for example—fairly began to flood the stage.

In Lope's time every university student studied the classics. Consequently, playwrights—most of whom were products of universities—turned in search of dramatic form to the Greeks, and especially to Aristotle. The Aristotelian formula was well known. Lope, however, departed from it to set a popular, nonclassic formula which Spain was to follow for many decades. (See Chapter 3.)

Sixteenth-century Spain had her Aristotle-oriented dramatists, but they failed to draw at the box office. Theirs was a wobbly position and Lope knew it, for Spaniards harbored an overwhelming predilection for action-filled plots over the slower-paced plots based on Aristotle's dramatic theories derived from Greek drama.

At the time of Lope de Vega's birth (1561), the most popular playwright in Spain was Lope de Rueda, who died in 1565. Since during most of his lifetime there were no permanent theaters, he barnstormed from town to town, performing on carts and portable platforms. Lope de Rueda wore three hats—of author, actor, and producer—and earned himself a national reputation. Cervantes himself paid tribute to him. Custom permitted the appearance of actresses on the stage. Lope de Rueda, in his latter years (to his sometime regret) married a young actress from his own company.

Alternating between prose and verse, Lope de Rueda wrote and produced full-length plays as well as one-act skits called *pasos*. Today these skits excite more interest than the plays they used to accompany, sandwiched in between (or before) the acts. The *pasos* are funny, folkish, anecdotal, realistic, primitive. Their characters are shepherds, half-wits, students, Negroes, farmers, Basques. Some speak their lines in dialect, an unfailing source of humor then as now, when artfully employed. Spain was and is rich in dialects. A principal merit of these skits is their liveliness of dialogue; another is their portrayal and satirization of human folly—although never in depth. The two best-known *pasos* are *The Planting of the Olive Trees* and *The Land of Cockaigne.*

A contemporary nearer Lope de Vega's age than Lope de Rueda was Seville-born Juan de la Cueva, (1550–1610?). On occasion this dramatist chose his subject matter from the classics, but principally he mined Spanish national history and tradition. Toward the end of his career he composed a manual for playwrights in which he urged his contemporaries to do as he had done and bring Spanish history and tradition, "the ingenious fable of Spain," ("la ingeniosa fábula de España"), to life on the stage. He thumbed his nose at the three unities and enthusiastically crusaded for a mixture of the comic and the tragic. Cueva wrote some fourteen dramas of which *The Seven Princes of Lara, The Siege of Zamora,* and *Bernardo del Carpio* are best known. All three are based on Spanish ballads.

Lope de Vega considered the Valencian Guillén de Castro y Bellvís (1569–1631) such a good friend that he dedicated a play to him, and Castro returned the favor by dedicating the first edition of his works to Lope and a play to his daughter, Marcela the nun. There is little certain knowledge of Castro's life. He was a soldier turned dramatist, a poet, and the author of a slender treatise on *How to Make Women Like You (Como han de granjearse las damas).* Evidently he failed to follow his own advice, since he left such misogynic comments as, "Oh, matrimony, heavy, violent yoke, if you were not a sacrament, I should say you are a demon," and "Who suffers worse than I from matrimony?" Once he was accused of hiring an assassin to commit a murder but was cleared of the charges. He took part in the popular poetry contests of the day, and on one occasion collaborated with eight other playwrights to write a play.

Guillén de Castro employed a variety of subjects in his plays: Biblical material, history, mythology, contemporary custom, and novels. He was the first Spanish playwright to dramatize *Don Quixote* and the first to dramatize the stories of Spain's national hero—the Cid—for the stage, in a two-part play called *The*

*Young Cid* (*Las mocedades del Cid*). In Paris Corneille adapted the second of these two plays to the taste of seventeenth-century France, giving France the capstone of her classic drama. The theme in both the Spanish and French plays is love versus duty, with duty sternly leading the protagonists down the road to tragedy. Lope spoke warmly of Castro's "lively genius." Some critics consider that Castro was too eager to use sensationalism for purposes of shock.

Friar Gabriel Téllez (1580?–1648), better known under the pseudonym of Tirso de Molina,[5] was so enthusiastic an admirer of Lope de Vega that he proudly declared himself in print to be his disciple and promised to defend his "new art" of playwriting against all comers, Aristotelian or Gongoristic. Indeed, Tirso's characters generally surpass Lope's, showing less improvisation and haste.

Tirso de Molina's greatest creation (some critics doubt it is his) is *The Sevillian Immoralist* (*El burlador de Sevilla*). This play, which initiated the Don Juan theme, perhaps the most generative theme in art in modern times, not only attained immortality in its own right but had far-reaching influence on some of the world's greatest creative minds, among them Molière, Thomas Corneille, Mozart, José Zorrilla, Espronceda, Goldoni, Balzac, Mérimée, Lord Byron, George Sand, Rostand, Baudelaire, Flaubert, Verlaine, Pushkin, Bernard Shaw, and nearly five hundred other writers and artists by actual count. (See Leo Weinstein, *The Metamorphoses of Don Juan*, Stanford University Press, 1959, pp. 187–214.)

One of Tirso's historical dramas, *Woman's Ingenuity* (*La prudencia en la mujer*), portrays a mother who heroically defends her son, Prince Ferdinand, during his minority, against vicious palace intrigues. Against formidable odds she brings him safely to the throne of his deceased father. One disquieting counter-reformational drama, *The Man Condemned for Little Faith* (*El condenado por desconfiado*), very probably by Tirso, stars a murderous thug saved from hell by faith and last-minute repentance, and costars his counterpart, a hermit condemned to hell through unbelief. The parallel with the thief on the Cross is apparent. Tirso, himself a priest, epitomized in this work the great issue of faith versus doubt, a question dear to the heart of the Spain of the three Phillips. This same Tirso, an erstwhile dealer in such weighty matters, created some of the naughtiest women characters of the century; namely, Martha in *Martha the Pious Hypocrite* (*Marta la piadosa*), built upon a current proverb; and Magdalena in *The Bashful Young Man in Madrid* (*El vergonzoso en palacio*). Furthermore his comedians were beyond a doubt the century's most vulgar. Tirso claimed to have written around four hundred plays, plus other literary items including a history of the Mercedarian monks (his religious order) and a book of short stories. This claim may be overstated.

The least prolific, but technically perhaps the most meticulous, playwright of the era was Juan Ruiz de Alarcón (1581?–1639), born in Mexico, and educated there and in Spain. He left only about twenty-four plays. He was a hunchback, and his contemporaries, including Lope de Vega, never let him forget it, scrawling grossly sarcastic verse about his deformity. Alarcón was very much the reformer and left a number of thesis plays which censure common human follies, such as calumny in *The Walls Have Ears* (*Las paredes oyen*), ingratitude in *Fairweather Friend* (*Mudarse por mejorarse*), and lying in *Truth Suspected* (*La verdad sospechosa*). The latter play, his masterpiece, was admired greatly and adapted to the French by Corneille, who said he would have swapped any two of his own works for it. Its main character is a young college graduate from Madrid who is in every sense a complete gentleman except for one defect of character: he is a compulsive liar. Alarcón built the intriguing action of the play around the confusion that evolves out of this youth's string of lies, moralistically punishes him in the end by forcing him to marry a woman (Lucretia) whom he does not love. In *The Liar* (*Le Menteur*) Corneille has the youth's affections turn gradually to Lucrèce, avoiding the shock of the forced marriage found in Alarcón's *Truth Suspected*.

But Alarcón did not always handle subject matter conservatively and realistically. In his *Antichrist*, (*El anticristo*) and *The Weaver of Segovia* (*El tejedor de Segovia*), he dispelled all restraint in theme and action. *The Antichrist* pulls out all the stops of Old Testament stories of fear, dread and consternation, false prophets, screams, devils, and black magic. *The Weaver of Segovia* offers nine-tenths of the characteristics later found in nineteenth-century European Romantic dramas, although Catholic faith still repressed religious doubt.

The kind of barbs Alarcón suffered in life were not spared him even in death. A reporter wrote, "Deceased: Juan Ruiz de Alarcón, a poet who achieved as much fame for his drama as for the hump on his back." A proud and áristocratic man, he loathed the common herd, denouncing it on one occasion as a "wild beast." To Lope and his other tormentors he returned their scathing jibes in kind.

Pedro Calderón de la Barca (1600–81), usually called simply Calderón, was and is the strongest rival of Lope de Vega for first place in Spanish drama. Born in Madrid, as were so many Spanish playwrights, Calderón went through the usual Jesuit school curriculum as a youth, studied at the universities of Alcalá and Salamanca, emerged with a scholastic, legalistic, and theological turn of mind. In his lifetime he incarnated the proverb "Young devil, old saint," leaving something of a record as a duelist (killing at least one opponent), soldier, and lover who fathered an illegitimate son before he settled down. Around middle age, like Lope de Vega, he became a priest; however, unlike Lope, he took the priesthood sufficiently in earnest to scotch wanton pleasure. He became a kind of palace poet in the Buen Retiro Theater of Felipe IV and after 1650 wrote plays only for the Courts, plays which were frequently pirated and produced elsewhere. Calderón was the recognized supreme master of the one-act Eucharistic play, called *auto sacramental*, and produced two or more a year until his death. His popularity remained extraordinarily constant through the centuries and probably no other playwright was so well known as he in the Spanish colonies; even Cervantes' name was hardly more universally known among the common people.

Calderón's variety of subject matter compares well with that of his contemporaries, including Lope de Vega. He borrowed from ancient, foreign, and national sources even though historical accuracy and local color were the least of his cares. He piled up anachronisms, repeatedly disregarded geography. His Greeks, Romans, Arabs and Englishmen—even his mythological personages such as Diana, Echo, and Narcissus—acted and reacted like Spaniards of his day in speech, psychology, passions, preju-

dices. He was seventeenth-century Spain's celebrated poet of
jealousy. His husbands killed their wives on suspicion of infidelity—as for example, *The Surgeon of His Own Honor* (*El
médico de su honra*) and *Secret Vengeance for Secret Insult* (*A
secreto agravio secreta venganza*). In his numerous cape-and-
sword plays he sought only to entertain with exciting suspense
and clever intrigue, lyrical love speeches, fancied danger for
young ladies, mistaken identity. He even stooped to slapstick,
as in such curtain raisers as *Flatulence* (*Los flatos*) and *Mr.
Snaggle-Tooth* (*El mellado*). His comics, textbook affirmations
to the contrary notwithstanding, were hilariously funny, and
sometimes even pornographic; e.g., Clarín and Moscón in *The
Prodigious Magician* (*El mágico prodigioso*), who querulously
share a maid between them on alternate days. The love speeches
Calderón redacted for young lovers, no matter how harrowing
the situation, were most appropriate and breathtakingly lovely.
His operas and vaudeville shows (*zarzuelas*) were supplied with
music by Spain's most noted musicians.

Calderón's dramatic masterpiece is *The Mayor of Zalamea* (*El
alcalde de Zalamea*) although he is better known abroad for *Life
Is a Dream* (*La vida es sueño*), his sole authentically philosoph-
ical play.

In *Life Is a Dream* Calderón argues hyperintellectually that
man is a beast but a beast who may triumph over his baser in-
stincts, and even over fate, by the use of reason, self-control, and
free will. More lyrical than logical in the conflicting doctrines
of this play, he outrages logic by the abuse of oxymoron. He
bewilders one, for example in *Life Is a Dream*, by crying "life is
a dream, and dreams are dreams," then further obfuscates by
providing that the protagonist, Prince Segismundo, alter his own
presumed fate.

Reason—or at least my reason—on reflection rejoins that if
a prediction can be changed, it may be a prediction, but it's not
fate. In *Life Is a Dream* astrology overflows and a profound
pessimism racks and scourges the protagonist, Prince Segismundo of Poland, through two and a half acts; only at the play's
violent finish does Segismundo see a glimmer of rather sober
optimism.

Calderón produced about one hundred and twenty plays in

addition to some eighty Eucharistic *autos sacramentales,* about twenty skits, numerous short musicals or vaudeville shows, and the librettos for an unknown number of operas. His *Daughter of the Air* (*La hija del aire*), in two parts, rivals Shakespeare's *The Tempest* for mystic poetic charm and philosophic substance. Few if any of his contemporaries mastered the use of allegory as he did in his Eucharistic plays, and none surpassed him in lyricizing—not even Lope. I return again and again to his poem on sleep in *Belshazzar's Feast* (*La cena del Rey Baltasar*), the Spanish language's counterpart to Macbeth's "the innocent sleep, sleep that knits up the ravelled sleave of care, the death of each day's life. . . ."

Following the obfuscating Gongoristic poetic style of his day, Calderón endeavored to dazzle with baroque passages that are ornate, bombastic, lavish, and bursting with conceits. In some of these he called a ship a comb combing the ocean's locks (foam), spoke of "hot snow," "cold fire," and "living corpses." Calderón relished puns and frequently expected his audience to take them seriously. He abused antithesis and often had too nice a plot balance, a plot too mathematically structured to be *vraisemblable,* as in *The House with Two Doors* (*Casa con dos puertas*).

Assisted by Cosme Lotti, the Cecil De Mille of the seventeenth century, Calderón staged costly extravaganzas, really grand spectacle, whose costs were borne by Felipe IV's bankrupt treasury.

At his best, Calderón surpassed all other Spanish dramatic poets of his day, including Lope de Vega.[6]

When Francisco de Rojas Zorrilla (1607–48) was three years old, his parents moved from Toledo, his birthplace, to establish residence in Madrid. As a child, Rojas Zorrilla lived near the homes of the most illustrious men of Spanish letters, including Cervantes and Lope de Vega, and not more than a few blocks from Spain's two principal theaters, the Príncipe and the Cruz, as well as near a popular loafing site (*mentidero*) for actors, painters, dramatists, directors, producers, and hangers-on. As a youth he went to college, but probably received no degree. By 1632, when he was twenty-five, he had already acquired some reputation as a dramatist and collaborated in playwriting with some of the great, including Calderón, from whom he learned much of his craftsmanship, including how to produce spectacle and extravaganza. In 1633, after the Buen Retiro Theater produced his dramatization of Cervantes' *Persiles and Segismunda,* Rojas Zorrilla caught Felipe IV's fancy and became firmly entrenched as a favorite Court dramatist. Within a short time seven of his plays were produced at the Buen Retiro, including his first tragedy, *One May Not be King and Parent* (*No hay ser padre siendo rey*). Like other Court playwrights, Rojas Zorrilla kept turning out entertainment for his royal patrons, comedy and tragedy flowing from his pen alternately, following each other kaleidoscopically. Periodically he presided over literary fun fests held to lampoon contemporary celebrities. On one occasion in 1638, Rojas Zorrilla was assaulted with murderous intent by a disgruntled poet whom Rojas had excoriated, and his injuries were so grave that reports went out he had died of his wounds. But he recovered, and during his convalescence wrote his masterpiece of humor, *The Game Is Up* (*Entre bobos anda el juego*), Ben Jonsonian in its humor. *The Game Is Up* rivals Molière's *The Would-be Gentleman,* is identical in technique with it: in *The Would-be Gentleman,* the single motive of the newly rich protagonist, M. Jourdain, is to become a fine gentleman; in *The Game Is Up,* the single motive of the vain protagonist, don Lucas, is to indulge his colossal vanity.

Like his contemporaries, Rojas could turn his hand successfully to drama of the somberest sort, and this he did in his approximately fifteen Eucharistic plays, and in his tragedies. In 1640 he was honored with a request to write a play for the opening of the lavish Coliseo Theater built for the king and courtiers. For the occasion he composed a spectacular based on the Romeo-Juliet theme, entitled *The Verona Feud* (*Los bandos de Verona*), produced by no less a sensational director than the above-mentioned Italian, Cosme Lotti, master of elaborate apparatus and sensational stage machinery.

Rojas coveted the Order of St. James. In time he attained the honor, but only after leaping over several hurdles and establishing an ancestral record of "clean blood" untainted by any Moorish or Jewish ancestry. In seventeenth-century Spain, racism was universally condoned by both church and state. As a result of this official attitude, a two-year-long investigation of Rojas' family records by government intelligence agents (spies) was instigated, but all it could ferret out was one onerous impediment to Rojas' qualifications for the honor: at one time his father had been a notary, an office formerly held in low esteem in Spain, as it had been centuries before in the "mother country" of Rome, where notaries were often slaves. Luckily the papal dispensation required to erase this stain was obtained.

Rojas wrote three plays on what might be called the theme of conflict between the generations, or father versus son; and five tragedies based on revenge as the chief motive, one of which used the story of Medea and Jason, and another the asp suicide of Cleopatra. He shook his contemporaries considerably by having women redress their own wrongs done them by men.

The most stirring and lyrical of the dramas assigned to Rojas, based partly on a play by Lope de Vega, is *None Save the King Is My Superior* (*Del rey abajo, ninguno*). The protagonists are a successful gentleman farmer, García del Castañar, and his stunningly beautiful wife, Blanca. The plot is old hat—mistaken identity—for García mistakenly thinks the king has sneaked into his wife's bedroom, whereas the culprit was in reality a courtier named don Mendo. Yet Rojas' poetry is so intensely lyrical at the moments of intensest grief or joy that the identity mixup on which the plot depends seems perfectly acceptable. During the better part of two acts the audience experiences the horrors a man feels where he thinks he must kill the woman he loves because he believes she has been dishonored by the king, whose person is sacred. And in the final thrilling scene of the play, a moment after García has slain the guilty don Mendo in a duel, Rojas epitomizes Spanish pride in a never-to-be forgotten scene of a subject standing proud and erect before his king, declaring, as if he spoke for all Spaniards, that ". . . as long as this neck rests on these shoulders, no one, from the King on down, shall offend my honor":

> . . . en tanto que mi cuello
> esté en mis hombros robusto,
> no he de permitir me agravie,
> del Rey abajo, ninguno.

The final line reiterates a proverb and consequently compounds the line's significance for the audience by its ringing familiarity.

The plays once assigned to Rojas Zorrilla exemplify another of the paternity snarls common in seventeenth-century drama. The scholar who has done most to unsnarl these paternities is Professor Raymond R. MacCurdy, who recently reduced the number of plays assignable to Rojas from eighty-seven to about thirty-five surely his alone, with fifteen additional plays written in collaboration.[7]

Another successful contemporary of Lope is Agustín de Moreto y Cabaña (1618–69). His parents were Italian property owners in Madrid at the time of his birth, and they saw to it that their son received a good education. We do not know what he looked like. In 1642 he took minor orders. Some years later he was active in caring for the poor and wretched in Toledo, and it was there that he made a will directing that his money go to the poor on his death, and that he be buried among them.

How many plays did Moreto write? No one knows for certain. One scholar, Ruth Lee Kennedy, in *The Dramatic Art of Moreto*,[8] assigns him only thirty-two plays written alone and eighteen written in collaboration. Other scholars have been more generous in their figures. We may classify Moreto's drama roughly as follows: one-act skits (*entremeses*); religious drama (such as *San Franco de Sena* about a bad man saved and converted to a saintly life); historical drama; situation comedies; and his most successful dramatic device—comedies of character motivated by some flagrantly extravagant eccentricity—such as vanity in *Don Diego the Dude* (*El lindo don Diego*), or assumed anthropophobia in *Answer Scorn with Scorn* (*El desdén con el desdén*).

In *El lindo don Diego* don Diego is a fop, convinced that all women fall in love with him on sight; he is also a fool who is tricked into marrying a servant girl, evidently with the assent of the audience, judging by the play's closing words: "And now this fool is punished to the satisfaction of the public. . . ." The plot of *El lindo* is engineered by a comedian named Mosquito. By Moreto's day comedians had become so popular in Spain that a number of Spanish playwrights, including Moreto, elevated them to the position of protagonists.

One play with this device was *Answer Scorn with Scorn*. This Moreto play features the comedian above all other characters in the play and became one of the most popular plays of all time in Spain and one of the most influential abroad. *Answer Scorn with Scorn* tells the story of the wooing of a haughty beauty, Diana, daughter of the Count of Barcelona, high in social station and rich, by young Carlos, whose every move is engineered by his servant, Moth (Polilla). Since childhood Diana has been inclined toward literature and learning in preference to men. Nevertheless many suitors have courted her and flattered her Dianaesque vanity. Carlos, contrary to the other suitors, declares unequivocally that he shares her scorn for love. Next he outpaces her by expressing a truculent desire not only never to love any woman, but never to be loved. But it is all a scheme, a part of Moth's campaign to bring Diana down in unconditional surrender. This play was perhaps the sexiest of the century: in one scene, Diana, in desperation teases Carlos with singing and dancing and all the undress the law allows. Without Moth's support, Carlos would weaken and blurt out his capitulation to Diana's seductive beauty and thereupon lose the game by default; but Carlos steadies himself and eventually brings Diana to a position of ultimate surrender: she proposes to him.

There is in *Answer Scorn with Scorn* a general resemblance to three different plays of Lope de Vega and to one play of Tirso de Molina; but these resemblances in no way detract from its originality, its wit, its tongue-in-cheek charm. Diana is as original as Shakespeare's Portia and quite as interesting. Moreto spun a sparkling comedy from a hackneyed theme. His Diana easily leaped over language barriers. A few years after *Answer Scorn with Scorn* appeared in Spain, Louis XIV, who had a Spanish wife, requested that Molière write a French version of it. He did and the result was *La Princesse d'Élide*. Moreto's Diana soon diverted audiences also in Italy and Germany. Years later (1825) she appeared in England in a translation entitled *Love's Victory, or The School for Pride,* by George Hyde.

Moreto mined the immense vein of Lope de Vega for plots and characters. He took his idea for *It Can't Be Done* (*No puede ser*) concerning the futility of attempting vigilance over women from Lope's *The Greatest Impossibility* (*El mayor imposible*), adapted by Crown to English as *Sir Courtly Nice, or It Cannot Be.* Moreto based *Honor First* (*Primero es la honra*) on Lope's

*The Law Obeyed* (*La ley ejecutada.*) Moreto's use of the works of other playwrights is so notorious that the Encyclopaedia Britannica labeled him a "brilliant plagiarist." This judgment is fair from the point of view of today's laws of copyright, but one ought to recall, before finally judging Moreto's borrowing, that he lived in an age of mutual pillaging, imitation, and just plain literary theft.

Lesser known playwrights contemporary with Lope de Vega are listed below:

Rey de Artieda (1549–1613)
Cristóbal de Virués (1550–1609)
Mira de Amescua (1574?–1644)
Vélez de Guevara (1579–1644)
Quiñones de Benavente (d.1652)
Jerónimo de Cáncer y Velasco (d.1655)
Antonio Enríquez Gómez (1600–60)
Francisco Antonio de Monteser (d.1668)
Juan de Matos Fragoso (1608–89)
Antonio de Solís y Rivadeneyra (1610–86)
Juan Vélez de Guevara (1611–75)
Antonio Coello y Ochoa (1611–82)
Sebastián Rodríguez de Villaviciosa (1618?)
Francisco de Avellaneda y la Cueva (1622?–1675?)
Juan de la Hoz y Mota (1622–1714)
Juan Bautista Diamante (1625–87)
Pedro Rosete Niño (?)
Los hermanos Figueroa y Córdoba (Diego y José) (?)

# CHAPTER 3

# Lope's Drama

I  *Classification—The Cosmos His Stage—How Many
Plays Did He Write?—Writing By Formula:*
The New Art of Playwriting (El arte
nuevo de hacer comedias)

EVERY writer who attempts to synthesize and interpret the
vast dramatic production of Lope de Vega feels dismay at
one time or another—sometimes panic. Where does one begin
to ladle out an ocean? How can one classify the seemingly un-
classifiable? By chronology? By author's apparent purpose? By
theme? Chronology will not serve as a basis because, in spite
of many efforts by people with intuitive hunches or by scholars
with IBM computers and "scientific" charts and graphs, the date
of composition of many works remain shaky. Author's purpose
as a basis, even if reasonably well identified, falls short of the
mark because the unmanageability of such a method complicates
classification beyond the point of returns. The traditional classification by theme, done some years ago by Marcelino Menéndez y
Pelayo, is still the one most frequently cited.[1]

My preference, in discussing Lope de Vega's drama, is to use
the protagonist's major characteristics as a basis of classification.
My reasons are two—to avoid classifying one play under more
than one heading, and to highlight the boundless range of Lope's
subject matter.

Inasmuch as a play's leading characters possess limited and
unmistakable characteristics which lend themselves to analysis
—and hence to classification—this premise supports my proposal
of a less obfuscating, single-entry system. Withal, such a system
highlights a neglected major fact about Lope: that he placed on
stage practically every type of being he ever met or heard about
or read about—from rogue to royalty, and thence even to deity
itself.

For the cosmos was his stage. In search of raw material for his drama, he roved from skid row to market place, to hidalgo's home, to palace, to church, to heaven, to hell. He presented to his audiences by the hundreds *pícaros,* the scum of the cities. He went down the social scale (and into jail, as a prisoner) scraping bottom to drag up jail birds, morons, bullies, bandits, pimps (male and female), whores, parasites, gigolos, and confidence men to write about. Spain swarmed with vagrants, often sarcastically called "thaumaturgic gents" (*caballeros de milagro*) because they had no visible means of support; these vagrants turned up in Lope's repertory, as did also astrologers, fortune tellers, degenerates, gangsters, beggars, friars, muleteers, Celestinas, and assassins for hire. He reviled the wicked, but exalted the "uncommon common man," whether from sincerity or from truckling to the crowd is a moot question. By contrast he portrayed counts, dukes, princes, queens, kings—he was among the first Spaniards who possessed the boldness to put royalty on the stage—and finally, going infinitely up the scale, he portrayed deity, both good and evil—God and the devil. Lope was bold, even reckless, in choosing his dramatic material, and even the sky was no limit, for he portrayed the separate members of the Holy Trinity, thereby soaring to a sort of cosmic plane of pride by putting words in the mouth of deity.

Lope looked for material everywhere, from sources ancient and contemporary, foreign and national, sacred and profane, pastoral, hagiographical, proverbial,[2] geographical, chivalresque. He moved across time and space. He found material familiar to his audiences in Spanish chronicles and in Spanish ballads and proverbs. He turned to Herodotus, Ovid, Horace, Boccaccio, Bandello, the *Celestina,* the Bible, and his predecessors in Spanish drama. Time and again he clothed in flesh and blood a mere proverb or a ballad character, or a national hero or heroine, whom his audience knew and loved or despised: this way he moved them as if they had seen the word become flesh before their eyes. He used overpowering emotional experiences from his own daily life: the fierce slap he gave Elena Osorio in a fit of jealousy, for example, appeared in Act III of *Motive Corrected* (*La intención castigada*).

With respect to Spain itself, Lope placed the proper mass man in the proper place. Character and place merged. He drenched himself with first hand knowledge of his fatherland. Instead of leaning on geography textbooks studied cursorily in his youth, Lope by traveling acquired knowledge of what is today called "human geography." He is thought to have matriculated at the University of Acalá at an early age.. Four or five years later he worked in Ávila, a walled city with a medieval spiritual as well as physical atmosphere. Seville, Cádiz, and Lisbon were next on his itinerary in 1582, and the Azores in 1583, with the armed forces of the Marquis of Santa Cruz, to put down a rebellion. In 1585, after having seen the inside of a jail in the company of his friend, Claudio Conde, he lived in Valencia (in exile from Madrid). Both men, along with Lope's brother, very likely went to Lisbon in 1588 to join the fleet (The Invincible Armada) against England. After 1588 Lope went to reside in Toledo, and for the next seven years periodically traveled, like a wandering tourist, with the ubiquitous Duke of Alba. The last year of the century found Lope secretary to the Marquis of Sarriá in Valencia. For Lope the seventeenth century opened with trips to Seville, Granada, and Antequera, and a return to Madrid in 1604. Then to Toledo, remaining until 1605; then back to Madrid where he began his twenty-five years of employment with the Duke of Sessa, himself something of a traveler. Before he died in Madrid in 1635, Lope had visited Burgos, Lerma, Ventosilla, Segovia, Toledo, Ávila, Alava, Guipúzcoa, the frontier between France and Spain (for a royal marriage), the high, dry plains of Old Castile, the Covarrubias mountain range, the mountains of León, the plains of Salamanca, Barcelona, Zaragoza, and many other places in Spain as well.

Lope knew well the characteristics of Spaniards of such greatly differing temperaments as the industrious Basques, the gabby and *simpaticos* Andalusians, the lean and austere Castilians, the dreamy Valencians, always singing. He learned at first hand how Spain was a bizarre mixture of *patrias chicas,* "little fatherlands," with all the contradictions that this situation embodied.[3] He observed Spain's classes and its castes, its bricklayers and its magistrates, its sociology and its psychology, its day-life and its night-life, its courtesans and its nuns, its pride and its corruption, its tenant farmers and its big-city wheeler-dealers. His observations were so broad and numerous that Sr. del Arco collected material for a volume of nine hundred pages on seventeenth-century Spanish society out of Lope's works, yet had a mountain of information left over.[4] If in another chapter we stared with disbelief at the extent of Lope's literary sources, we stare likewise at his knowledge of Spain's land and its people.[5] One has the impression that he moved about constantly on the lookout for dramatic types and that he had total recall of peoples and places, judging by reflection on the speech of his characters about cities, harbors, villages, landmarks, castles, inns, roads, and ships.

Lope manifested particular affection for everything nonurban: country landscapes, country towns, country people, country food. In *The Farmer's Home Is His Castle* ( *El villano en su rincón* ) Lope built up such a lyrical series of rustic scenes that city life seems worsted for all time. Of course, he knew first hand the age-old classic debate of country life versus city life and was influenced by it, but his praise of country ways and country people was too extensive and frequent to be other than primarily based on actual experience. The corruption of Madrid, the city he knew best, caused him to develop ambivalent feelings toward her. He looked affectionately upon Madrid. Yet her many flaws made him yearn for country life.

Madrid, a great world capital, where he spent most of his life, swarmed with an enormously heterogenous population of strangers, foreigners, poachers, parasites and other nonproductive transients. Estimates were made that the number of transients in Madrid was forty thousand, among whom were spies for foreign governments, French and Italian bullies, and swarms of Spanish vagrants, *pícaros,* and pimps. Lope once said in a letter to the Duke of Sessa that the streetwalkers of Madrid were complaining at the competition given them by the sodomites. Lope never wrote picaresque novels featuring the lowly and miserable, but he put on stage numerous characters with spiritual texture resembling Lazarillo de Tormes or Guzmán de Alfarache, and often his plays were quite as episodic as picaresque literature and reflected picaresque humor. He had explored Spain's principal cities and knew many a skid row (el Compás in Sevilla, el Potro in Córdoba, for example), each a haven for thieves, pickpockets, bullies, galley slaves, panderers, and transient whores. Here the *germanía* (jargon of gypsies and thieves) flourished and renewed itself, and here Lope learned skid row thought with its picturesque language of wretchedness.

Like his predecessor, the primitive dramatist Lope de Rueda, and his contemporary, Shakespeare, Lope de Vega gave comic relief by drawing on the limitless reservoir of the masses. Where appropriate he used their folkish dialect. He especially drew *graciosos* (comedians) from out of this commonality. These were usually cowardly, poor, untrustworthy, stupid, or canny types, as the case might require—models of go-thou-and-do-not-likewise. "Honor and pride," asks a *pícaro* in *The Grand Duke of Russia* (*El Gran Duque de Moscovia*), "what the hell are *they* good for in this world?"

The source of much of Lope's material is folklore. He absorbed vast amounts of what might be called *la filosofía vulgar* (the philosophy of the common man) and transformed it into theater. The psychology of the folk is ubiquitous. His esteem for proverbial wisdom was so great that he not only made hundreds of characters speak in proverbs, but he imitated the proverbial style and content, and even put Spanish proverbs into the mouth of deity itself. If one goes down the line of the categories of folklore, one finds Lope's mind and heart open to all of them: animal lore, plant lore, folk tales, folk songs, ballads, customs, beliefs, superstitions, prejudices, regional folk accents (for humorous effect), legends, traditions, foods, clothing, dances (including belly dancing).

Lope created a vast army of common people: farmers, millers, masons, day laborers, Negro slaves, spinners, charcoal burners, seamstresses, washwomen, cooks, scrub women. Hundreds of these characters are on the distaff side, usually ravishing without benefit of the beauty-salon aids available to women of rank.

> Some peasant girls,
> without makeup and fancy clothes,
> bear away our eyes
> and with them our hearts.
> —*The King the Greatest Alcalde*, Act I

> Hay algunas labrodoras
> que, sin afeites ni galas,
> suelen llevarse los ojos,
> y a vuelta de ellos el alma.
> —*El mejor alcalde, el Rey*, Act I

Lope turned often to the hidalgo for characters. He took his material from observation in streets and plazas and churches and parks and in private homes, particularly in Madrid, Seville, Valencia, and Toledo. His dramas encompass and reflect fashions, fads, fiestas, masses, pilgrimages, minor characters returned after lengthy residence in the New World (the so-called *indianos*), snobs, show-offs, magistrates. All these and more will be found in Lope's cape-and-sword plays, or situation comedies. This type of play came from a spontaneous rather than a reflective Lope. With his cape-and-sword play he sought first and last to entertain, generally ignoring ethical objective.

Lope's women characters were usually superior to the men, being often gay, rebellious, energetic, courageous, even heroic. The men considered themselves *caballeros*, were slaves to honor (see Chapter 3, Section II, on Spanish honor), hotheaded, proud, idle, and on the prowl for sexual adventure. But Lope turned so often to the hidalgo class for subject types that he boiled the same cabbage over and over. The reader of cape-and-sword plays finds himself thumbing back to the cast of characters in order to distinguish between Juan and Antonio, or Félix and Fernando. Worse still, Lope repeatedly oversimplified his characters—a practice which today seems downright primitive because our century is convinced of the meaningfulness of every aspect of thought and conduct, of the radically unfragmented and untrivial character of everything a man does—or doesn't—do. There is fairly general belief that all mental activity, conscious or unconscious, normal or abnormal, is drenched in meaning. The generally approved oversimplified discrimination between the trivial and the significant of Lope's day is gone. We are accustomed to a kind of "realism" which demands that playwrights attempt to be verisimilar and logical, justify every motive, action, movement—and analyze, analyze, analyze. In short, our realism demands a sort of *clinicalism* on which we have constructed our critical standards. Hence with such a frame of reference, we're likely to conclude that, with the exception of their vigorously thoughtful analysis of love, or logic-chopping over points of honor, plays like *The Iron Tonic of Madrid* (*El acero de Madrid*), *The Dog in the Manger* (*El perro del hortelano*), *The Nightmarish Night* (*La noche toledana*), and *The Power of Scorn* (*Los milagos del desprecio*), offer quite primitive fare.

These numerous plays about hidalgos provide a rare *olla podrida* (Spanish stew). Into them Lope poured humor, a variety of minor types, disguises, masked men, veiled women, criss-crossed intrigue, startling effects, women sensually dressed in men's clothing (cf. Shakespeare's *Twelfth Night*), surprises aborted out of coincidence, *Schicksaldrama* (fate tragedy), rapid succession of incident making plays often seem episodic, risqué scenes of hiding in bedrooms and attics, mistaken identity, eavesdropping, and great emphasis on action. A representative play is *The Iron Tonic of Madrid* (*El acero de Madrid*), which features two lovers outmaneuvering an obnoxious and watchful Aunt Theodora, the young heroine by pretending illness, the young hero by impersonating a physician. Another is *The Dog in the Manger* (*El perro del hortelano*), featuring the wealthy Countess of Belflor who repeatedly refuses a young man's offer of marriage, all the while jealously forbidding his marriage to a rival. The youth only succeeds in curing her of her dog-in-the-manger complex by the use of strong measures in the final act.

Other action-filled plays featuring the hidalgo class of Lope's day are *The Power of Scorn* (*Los milagros del desprecio*), *Pretty Ugly-Duckling* (*La hermosa fea*), and *Miss Simpleton* (*La dama boba*). This latter play, built on the theme that "love cures all," including a low I.Q., is enormously amusing. It is superior on many counts to its twentieth-century counterpart, *Born Yesterday* (with the late Judy Holliday), the most successful Hollywood adaptation ever made on the theme of "love-the-physician."

When Lope de Vega initiated the practice in Spain of putting royalty on the stage, it turned out to be a sure-fire device. He thrilled his audiences by presenting in the flesh a Visigothic king, or Jaime el Conquistador, or Pedro the Cruel, or the big favorites, Ferdinand and Isabella. Occasionally Lope gave audiences Moorish royalty—usually to be hissed at, of course. He chose royal personages from Biblical and classical times down through the centuries to his own day, not excepting Felipe II, III, and IV. Just as Americans who see Lincoln in a play or movie respond emotionally to their own personal image of him, so the Spanish responded to their mental image of past kings and other historical and traditional celebrities who had left their stamp on ballad, song, tale, anecdote, or proverb. As with Shakespeare, among Lope's kings and princes one finds strong rulers and weak, good and wicked, colorful and colorless. An example of a concerned, just, *simpatico* king is Alfonso VII in *The King the Greatest Mayor* (*El mejor alcalde, el rey*). Alfonso made himself available to his humblest subjects, especially if they were from his own native region of Galicia. Highlighted in the play is a ruthless, petty feudal lord, Don Tello, far removed from court; he arrogantly stopped a rustic wedding, abducted the beautiful bride, Elvira, and took her to his castle. Sancho, the bridegroom, journeyed the long distance to court, obtained the King's order to the tyrant to restore the bride unharmed. But in vain. Don Tello thumbed his nose at royal authority. So Sancho repeated the tedious journey to court. King Alfonso, seeing his authority defied, himself returned incognito with Sancho to Tello's domain to do justice. After collecting positive proof of Tello's crime, he called ominously for a "priest and a hangman." Dramatically Elvira entered with clothes torn and hair disheveled, the kind of scene Lope relished. She poured out her grief in moving lines of poetry addressed to his Majesty the King. She had not given in to Tello, bribery and cajolery notwithstanding. But he had forced her into the woods and assaulted her. King Alfonso married her on the spot to Tello, had the executioner chop off his head, and gave as her dowry half of the just deceased's large estate to the newly made widow. A curtain then was drawn to disclose the theatrical company's stock papier-mâché head. Justice had been done, monarchy exalted. Even though Alfonso VII had relatively few lines to speak, Lope portrayed him as the possessor of such regal dignity as to appear the epitome of princeliness equally for today's reader as for the seventeenth-century theatergoer.

Lope wrote many plays featuring royalty. A favorite pair of monarchs of his host of fans were Ferdinand and Isabella, whom Lope always portrayed sympathetically; for example, *Spain's Fairest Son* (*El mejor mozo de España*), 1610, in which he transported his audience back in time to the final unhappy days of Henry (Enrique) IV's reign. He depicted the young and beautiful Princess Isabella at the spinning wheel, living in peaceful rustic surroundings. But the supernatural intervened. She fell into a sleep, saw Spain lying prone on the earth, dressed in mourning, bewailing sorrowfully her dreadful condition but prophesying that Isabella would lift her up again. A little later Isabella received the news of the death of her brother and rival for the throne, Alfonso, leaving the road to the throne unobstructed when King Henry should die. But trouble came when Henry followed one of his whims and ordered Isabella not to marry as long as he remained alive; however, the nobility thought that she should marry, and the search for a husband began. Conflict arose from these differences of opinion. Isabella received what appeared to be instructions from on high that her husband should be Ferdinand of Aragon, who also wanted a royal spouse. The problem then became how to outmaneuver King Henry, who closed his borders to Ferdinand. Ferdinand disguised himself as a mule driver, instructed his inferiors to treat him as if he were a servant, and after many a danger, reached Isabella, herself now disguised as a farm girl. They fell in love at first sight and were married. The beautiful actress who portrayed Spain in mourning now reappeared, her black clothes cast off for brighter ones; treading upon her enemies, she closed the act by prophesying the future greatness of the reign of Ferdinand and Isabella. One can hear the spontaneous applause of the audience patriotically stirred on seeing 100 per cent Apostolic-Roman-Catholic Hispanicism triumphant (once again) on the stage.

Lope de Vega never hesitated to place anything he fancied in a play. If he portrayed conquistadors, who were "supermen" of the secular world, he also portrayed saints, who were "supermen," in a manner of speaking, of the spiritual world. He assigned them characteristics taken from the *Flower of Saints*

(*Flos Sanctorum*), the *Golden Legend* (*Legenda Aurea*), and from popular lore, thus catering to the popular taste. He displayed his enthusiasm for saints by composing more than twenty-five *comedias* about them, adding voluminously to Roman-Catholic literature. He used saintly characters to preach Catholic dogma, countering the Reformation and other "heresies." He felt with the people that saints were as heroic as soldiers and conquistadors.

Lope de Vega was clearly a reformer who, in spite of his irregular personal life, was trying to reform Spaniards by acquainting them with the lives of men who presumably were attempting to imitate Christ on earth. But because of the undramatic nature of the subject matter, he was generally unsuccessful in this endeavor. For the most part his saints' plays may be classed with his worst failures. They were usually plotless, episodic, superficial, too close to popular devotion—comedies of magic, with superficial characterization, angels, miracles, devils, stage devices, startling effects.

Lope injected theological debates into saints' plays, but always cautiously remained within the strict bounds set by the Spanish Inquisition. He showed a sort of cosmic naïveté, especially in the plays where he paraded on stage up to sixteen saints, including the Holy Family. He made his saints' plays more like pageants than dramas, and on occasion put in as many as eighty-five characters, as for example in *John of God and Antón Martín* (*Juan de Dios y Antón Martín*). He placed, side by side with people, personified abstractions, such as Falsehood, Envy, and Original Sin, as was common practice in the allegorical Eucharistic (*auto sacramental*) religious play. The latter was of one act, the saints' play usually of three. But Lope evidently hoped to set before his Spanish audience all "final" metaphysical solutions to life's problems, and to attack the heresies of the Jews, Moors, Albigensians, Arians, Manicheans, pagan Romans, astrologers, and especially the Protestants (*luteranos*). The latter he pointedly labeled "diabolical." He treated certain doctrines right on the stage: the Holy Trinity, the Christian plan of salvation, the efficacy of last-minute repentance, transubstantiation, purgatory, eternal torment.

Among the saints he portrayed were Mary, Joseph, Augustine,

Francis, Gabriel, Isidro, Adam, David, Zacharias, and many more. They came from both the Old and the New Testaments and from subsequent history. Mariology was particularly exalted. Most of the settings in the saints' plays were taken from the Bible, with Spain second, then Italy, North Africa, India, Portugal, and other countries in diminishing frequency. He assigned the saints all the personal virtues that one can imagine, such as humility, continence, innocence, hope, joy, knowledge of the Bible, discretion, faith, stability, piety, poverty, practicality, purity, resignation, simplicity, love of solitude, tenderness, radiance, all characteristics which Lope for the most part lacked, but pined for, and castigated himself for lacking. But the number of worthy qualities that Lope assigned to his saintly characters was so fabulous that they seem scarcely human at all. In dramatizing them he fell into contradictions, even absurdities. One saint wished to spare a tree in order to save the insects, little creatures of God; yet the same saint approved the bloody conflict of a religious war. Another saint referred to himself as dust, a sinner, a worm, yet declared humility was vanity. Still another labored with a woman to establish a religious order, never daring to look directly at her lest he be tempted. Lope was out of his depth with so much virtue.[6]

I have said that the cosmos was Lope's stage; so I come now to his *autos sacramentales,* for it is mostly in these one-act plays written to commemorate the Eucharist that he dared to portray deity, thus covering the full range of beings from bottom to top. But a few words about the nature of the *autos* and their significance in his day. They were Church approved for sound doctrine, of one act, written in verse, and were played on *carros* (platforms on wheels) in the public plazas nearly always to celebrate Corpus Christi. The municipality paid for their staging, which was lavish. They were seen first by royalty, then by the grandees of Spain, and finally by the common people. They were solemnly performed "to glorify the true faith." They had a long complex history springing from the Middle Ages, and they displayed their medieval origin in numerous ways, particularly in the use of allegory.

Eucharist plays became enormously popular during the seventeenth century, and Lope's younger contemporary, Calderón de la Barca, became the acknowledged leader in this genre. Eighteenth-century Spain outlawed them.

Lope wrote many. No one knows the number. Their themes came from the Bible, lives of saints, and even from secular sources. The characters frequently appearing were: Our Eternal Father, King of Heaven, Omnipotence, Divine Love, Jesus Christ (in differing guises, as Good Shepherd, a Crusader, the Bridegroom of the Church, etc.), the Virgin Mary, Mercy, Grace, Justice, Judaism, Heresy, Lucifer, Darkness (symbol of sin), Man, Reason, the Soul, Death, etc.[7]

In Lope's Eucharist plays time was scrambled, anachronisms abounded, Old Testament prophets appeared contemporary with the Apostles; but no matter, for the themes were timeless.

A favorite Lopean *auto sacramental* of mine is *The Voyage of the Soul* (*El viaje del alma*). Its plot is inconsequential: Soul goes on a wild voyage aboard the infamous ship "Delight" commanded by Captain Satan, but before the journey is finished she is persuaded to debark and board the good ship "Penitence," commanded by Christ and manned by a crew of angels. The play closes with an invitation to all to partake of the Lord's Supper and the mystery of transubstantiation.

Into this slender plot Lope worked a prodigious amount of subject matter, a sort of lyricized "instant Bible." He informed his audience (practically in a nut-shell) of the story of Creation and of God's plan of salvation; he prophesied Satan's return and the end of the world *in the twentieth century*, "proved" the prediction with Bible chronology; he spoke with poetic brevity to an audience clearly well versed in the Bible of Adam and Eve and Original Sin; of Cain and Abel, Seth, Enos; of the Flood, the Tower of Babel, Moses crossing the Red Sea; of Christ's arrival on earth, His miracles, His crucifixion, transubstantiation ("Man eats Him and deifies himself . . ."). And Lope somehow managed to mention, in whizzing by, the origin of France and Italy, with a few items from classical mythology, including for good measure Helen of Troy. He also compressed into this lyrical tour de force the belief that *Entendimiento* (Understanding) is the chief guide to Salvation, although he assigned the part to a censorious old man. He made Will something of a *gracioso*, prone to chase after pretty women and run with the Devil after Pleasure.

The dramatist's thesis in *The Voyage of the Soul* is Good and Evil struggling for the Soul. Of course, Evil is bested by Christ in the final scene, which highlights an elaborate chalice superbly made at inestimable cost ("de maravillosa labor a inestimable precio")—for the Lord's Supper. (The marginal notes on the manuscript of the play indicate that "only sound doctrine" was used.)

Also compressed along the way into this digest of the Bible were music and dancing, a bit of obscure baroque verse, a touch of humor, a highly lyrical narration of Soul's repentance, an unsanctimonious and exceedingly lively (but untranslatable) lyrical shanty, ("¡Hola! Que me lleva la ola, ¡Hola! Que me lleva la mar"), and a very folksy verse to highlight the Lord's Supper.

| | |
|---|---|
| On this divine table, | En esta mesa divina, |
| Beloved, if you are in grace | Carillo, si estás en gracia, |
| Play, sing, eat and drink, | Tañe, canta, come y bebe, |
| Leap, eat, and dance and dance. | Salta, come, danza, y baila. |

Finally, it would be a careless omission to neglect to say that the ship's Captain, Christ, is heard to speak in technical marine vocabulary! Both Lope and his audience knew their ships as well as their Bible.

Lope de Vega nearly always wrote with a sort of mass man perspective toward all things, even when he composed Eucharist plays. He placed dancing and singing shepherds and shepherdesses, some of whom spoke a folkish dialect, in *The Return from Egypt* (*La vuelta de Egipto*). He put tavern scenes, muleteers, unprincipled innkeepers, wranglers and brawlers, and a bloody youth grasping a dagger all in *The Tyrant Punished* (*El tirano castigado*), along with characters speaking the lyrical poetry about Christ's birth and the "Magnificat" of Saint Mary, the canticle she spoke to her cousin, Elizabeth (Luke 1: 46–56).

Lope made these plays fit the thought patterns of religiosity of the masses.[8] The psychology of the folk is felt everywhere. Clearly he was also trying to be an innovator in this vastly popular Eucharistic segment of drama. With these religious plays Lope reached his zenith in choice of character, although not in his art, by ascending to deity. City slums to the heavens: the cosmos was his stage, though he saw it through the eyes of a seventeenth-century Spaniard and portrayed it most often as viewed by the common man.

Only Lope's vast range of subject matter rescued his plays (at least in his day) from the blight of formula monotony.

HOW MANY PLAYS DID LOPE DE VEGA WRITE? The question of Lope's dramatic production is a nest of nettles. "He [Lope] by himself alone wrote more in quantity and quality than all the poets ancient or modern . . . The number of his plays put on in the theater was 1,800. He also wrote more than 400 one-act Eucharistic plays, and numerous books and papers . . ." This is the assertion of Dr. Pérez de Montalbán (in 1636), a disciple and friend of Lope. The playwright himself claimed one hundred plays written at the production rate of one in twenty-four hours. One of the best known Lope scholars, Emilio Cotarelo y Mori, writing in 1935, asserted zealously that this large figure is unshakable and incontrovertible. And in defending Lope's "supernatural fecundity" he gives no quarter to doubting Thomases, confidently maintaining that sober evidence overwhelmingly favors 1,800 plays.[9] Quoting the figures on Lope's production given by Lope's contemporaries and by Lope himself, Cotarelo formulated the following table:

| Year | Number of Plays Claimed for Lope |
|------|----------------------------------|
| 1604 | 300 |
| 1609 | 483 |
| 1618 | 800 |
| 1620 [10] | 900 |
| 1625 | 1,070 |
| 1631 | 1,500 |
| 1635 | 1,800 |

Sr. Cotarelo maintains that not more than 520 of Lope's plays survived, that more than two-thirds were lost, in great part because of the enmity of drama-despising moralists, especially those Jesuit fathers who thundered against attendance at the theater, against having copies of plays in the home, and against actors and actresses, whom they considered unworthy of receiving the holy sacraments. (In seventeenth-century France actors were denied burial in holy ground. So were they in Spain, but the decree was not always followed.) One highly esteemed Jesuit father descended to hell to find hyperboles for condemning playwrights in general, and Lope in particular. In 1631 he thundered out that "this Lope de Vega has written more than 1,000 plays and published 2 volumes of them, thereby causing more sin in the world than 1,000 devils." The state, too, periodically passed laws hampering the production and printing of plays, and the death of a monarch might mean closed theaters throughout the realm for months at a time. Through the centuries accident, chance, and the combined enemies of the theater thus managed to destroy two-thirds of Lope's drama, according to Cotarelo.[11]

Using more or less identical evidence concerning the number of Lope's plays, but seeking out discrepancies impassively, Professors S. G. Morley and Courtney Bruerton in 1935[12] came up with a greatly reduced figure, far under eighteen hundred.[13] They question just how much faith should be put in the words of Lope and his friends. For one thing, Lope, like Cervantes and others of his age, is known to have used numbers as he might use other adjectives—as metaphors. In his sworn testimony before the Spanish court at the time of his trial for slander of the Velázquez family (not the painter) in 1587, Lope stated that he was "twenty-four years old, more or less." In reality he was twenty-five and four months old. In 1618 Lope's metaphorical use of round numbers demonstrated an intentional distortion of facts, for in this year he gives us both the figures of 462 and of 800 plays, "omitting many I don't remember."

In other years, too, we find similar discrepancies in Lope's use of numbers. Round numbers were the order of the day, however careless this practice may seem to the age of IBM, statistics, and charts and graphs. Contemporaries of Lope use similar approximations; for example, Luis Vélez de Guevara said in 1637, "hartos (consonates de sangre) he sudado en 400 comedias que he hecho." ("I have sweated out a plethora of laborious rhymes in the 400 plays I have written"). His extant plays number only about eighty-five. Another case of similar loose assertion is the monk-playwright Tirso de Molina (pen name of Gabriel Téllez), creator of the Don Juan legend, who in the early years of the seventeenth century mentioned casually the "three hundred plays which in fourteen years have diverted me from boredom and palliated idleness." His extant plays number some eighty. "Is the word of the monk [Tirso] more to be trusted than that of the priest Lope?" ask Professors Morley and Bruerton; "May we not hazard the guess that Tirso, who followed his admired master so closely in technique, imitated him also in boasting of his fecundity and in exaggerating it?"

Professors Morley and Bruerton conclude that eight hundred plays would be a generous allowance for Lope de Vega until further documentary evidence comes to light. Even this enormous number should be sufficient to establish him as a true "monstruo de la naturaleza" ("prodigy of nature"), as Cervantes nicknamed him. It certainly seems unnecessary for his admirers, even those who approach him on their knees, to represent as more prolific the prolific author of eight hundred plays.

WRITING BY FORMULA—THE NEW ART OF PLAY WRITING. What ever the number of Lope's plays, eight hundred or eighteen hundred, he had to write in a hurry. If you write in a hurry you must have a formula, and this formula must pay off at the box office. Lope had such a device, especially for his comedies of manners (*comedias de capa y espada*).

He left his formula to posterity. In it he tells us of some of the circumstances moral and physical, subject matter, gimmicks, dramatic tricks, and illusions he thought should be used. He called his formula *The New Art of Play Writing* (*Arte nuevo de hacer comedias*),[14] and read it before a Madrid literary society in 1609, being then no green and youthful beginner but a mature man of forty-seven, successful and famous, and long since past the forks of the road of choice of dramatic critical philosophy, Aristotelian versus popular, having chosen the latter.

The formula and stamp he put on Spain's national drama was enduring.

He had repeatedly survived paper wars fought in Madrid by the learned Aristotelian minority,[15] and he was once more fighting off their attacks in 1609.[16] The critic Menéndez Pelayo considered Lope's Madrid speech a recantation for having catered to the many.[17] Others interpret it as the declaration of a prodigy and a rebel carrying out one of the most thrilling ventures in modern times—the creation of a national drama.[18]

Like many predecessors, and like Boileau and Pope who followed him, Lope wrote his treatise in verse. In his very first stanza he addressed the gentlemen of the society sarcastically, saying he knew the classic rules of drama and had known them since he was a mere novice of ten, but he disregarded them because "the man who attempts to write according to rules known to so few people will fail financially. When I sit down to write a play, I lock up the rules with six keys and drive Plautus and Terence out of my study to stop their howling. I keep my eye on the box office, and because the common man pays the piper, I pipe the tune he likes."

Next Lope played the pedant and cited rather arrogantly a series of critical "authorities" out of the past for show-off effect, then made a U turn and outlined the formula needed, in his opinion, to please the common man: choose your subject, even kings and queens if they are called for (although King Felipe II disliked to see commoners pretend to be royalty); mix the comic and the tragic; keep a tight unity of action, but disregard the other two classic unities—time and place. Jump over time and speed the accomplishment of many years with an hourglass, especially when you write historical plays: the impatient Spaniards want to see the creation of the world and Doomsday, Genesis to Judgment Day, all in a couple of hours. Divide your play into three acts and keep suspense until the last, for "the minute the *mosqueteros* (standees) guess the ending of a play, they begin to look toward the exits."

Avoid an empty stage or your audience quickly gets restive. Use domestic language in domestic scenes, but when your character seeks to persuade, advise, or dissuade, use maxims and epigrams and wit. Avoid obscure, altisonant language. (A slap at his paper-war opponent, Góngora, advocate of obscurity in poetry.) Adjust the dialogue to fit the character: make kings speak with majesty, old men like old men, lovers with such passion that they transform the listeners. Keep proper decorum toward women. Dress them frequently in men's clothing, for this is all the rage. Try to make all things appear as probable and likely as possible (verisimilitude). Do not forget in Act III what you have already written in Act I. (He did forget in a number of plays.)

Use all the dramatic tricks of the drama trade, and "deceive with the truth." Use the correct verse form to fit the particular situation: those in waiting should speak in sonnets; the narrator in ballads; the speaker on somber subjects in tercets. Use *double-entendre* or puns frequently, for both feed the vanity of the common man, who prides himself in being the only one to catch their meaning. Use the honor theme often, for nothing is more universally liked. Keep satire subtle; don't "tell all"; put a little mystery in things. Use local color in costuming (a futile request, invariably disregarded by directors).

Lope criticized himself in jocular fashion for toadying to the common man, then wrote his penultimate stanza in Latin just to prove that he was as learned as the next man. He concluded his longiloquence with a coda written out of sheer vanity, in Spanish: "Listen . . . and don't be so contentious about *how* to write plays; you can learn all about it by going to the theater and just listening." In other words, "watch me."

*Peribáñez*, a play of country life, typifies Lope's most successful use of his formula: *three acts; theme: love* and *honor* (Peribáñez, a young farmer, the hero; Casilda, his wife, the heroine, with whom the youthful overlord falls in love); *Spanish local color* (the marriage fiesta; the celebration of the Assumption); *historical background* (the expeditionary force of Henry III of Castile, early fifteenth century); *characters from upper and lower classes* (royalty with its grandeur, the commander of royal armed forces, clowning servants, farmers); *a pompous retinue* (splendor of dress); *a variety of verse* (native Spanish and imitation of Italian forms); *several changes of scene* (in Ocaña and in Toledo); *passage of time, several days;* mixture of *comic and tragic; a "just" ending* (death of the guilty overlord and preservation of the honor of Peribáñez); *lyricism* throughout the play, especially highlighted at most dramatic moments (Casilda expressing her loving preference for Peribáñez over the wooing overlord); *use of balladry, singing, musical instruments, and dancing; plot based on a ballad:* "Más quiero yo a Peribáñez/ con su capa la pardilla,/ que al Comendador de Ocaña/ con la suya guarnecida." (My Peribáñez in his cheap, drab cape is more dear to me than the Governor of Ocaña with all his finery.) Lope following his formula in *Peribáñez* gave Spain one of its greatest plays.

Realizing early in his career that he had come upon a successful formula, Lope followed it more or less closely throughout his career. It helped to keep his family above the bread-and-butter line, no easy job for a writer in his or any time, especially in Spain. Classic drama would have led him over the hill toward, if not to, the poorhouse. So he sought out the popular formula that pleased the man in the street and stayed with it. Even so, he protested that he loathed the whole business. "The common man is paymaster and so . . . it's only fair to speak to him in the idiotic speech he likes." A character in *King Pedro in Madrid* (*El rey don Pedro en Madrid*) echoed, "Learn how to please the common people and you will achieve success." In this same mood of protest he once called his own verse "mercenary poetry." In Act I of *Justice Without Revenge* (*El castigo sin venganza*) he had a wise jester, Batín, say that "fame among the ignorant herd is not true fame"; in the same act a Duke sneers that "the common herd is no judge of truth; people are fools who base their good name on what crass minds believe. The rabble's opinions are inconstant and variable, not ruled by reason." Toward the end of his life Lope wrote in *Eclogue to Claudio* (Claudio was a close friend) of the sense of bitterness he felt toward the mass man and his degraded tastes: "I always truckled to the crowd for laughs and busied myself with a lot of love plots. . . . I should have been lucky enough to have had a Mecenas . . . but my luck was so bad that I had to write five large sheets (*pliegos*) every single day of my life in order to keep my head above water . . . and *in order not to offend my oppressor* [sic, meaning the "people"], *I could never write about anything that had genuine substance to it* . . ." (Italics added).

He clearly considered his drama to be outside the domain of art, and this attitude partly explains why he waited so late in his career to publish his plays. Many had already been printed without his authorization. In 1604, because poetasters were selling their own wares under his name, he printed a list of all the titles of his plays he could remember in *The Pilgrim in His Own Country* (*El peregrino en su patria*), but he omitted many.

II *Lope's Lyricism: From Experience to Verse—His Chauvinism—Honor, Reputation, and Face-Saving: Señoras and Señoritas on Precarious Pedestals.*

"In what work of Lope de Vega," asked Alonso Zamora Vicente, one of his biographers, "does one NOT find lyricism?" [19] Over and again, in the most unexpected places and situations, Lope catches us by surprise with a terse, lively, sharp, clean, fresh expression of a universal experience or emotion. I should like to quote a noteworthy example from *The Knight from Olmedo,* worthy in the original of being set beside the love speeches of Romeo and Juliet. Alonso is the hero of the play, Inés his beloved. Rodrigo is Alonso's rival for Inés' hand, and is favored by her father. Tello is the *gracioso*. One must remember how great the loss is when verse is translated into prose, though Jill Booty has done her translation with skill and understanding of both the situation and the language.

INÉS: Tello, my friend! . . .
TELLO: My queen!
INÉS: My dear Alonso, how your absence tortured me! Rodrigo has been here again.
ALONSO: Although obedience to your father may compel you to marry him, I will not abandon hope until I hear the sentence pronounced. I told Tello, even as he saddled our horses, that my heart was troubled and that my melancholy sprang from some new misfortune which as yet I had not heard. And now that I am with you, you tell me that it is so. Alas, for me if it prove true!
INÉS: Do not believe it, dear my lord, for I will say "no" to all the world, having given my word to you. You alone are master of my life and my will. There is no power on earth, Alonso, that can force me from my course, which is to be your wife. In the empty hours of yesterday, I beguiled the time by walking in the garden

alone. As I wandered, I told my love to the fountains and to the flowers, and as I did so the tears ran down my cheeks. "Fountains and flowers," I said, for so I spoke in my loneliness, "you enjoy a happy life, for although the night may come to shroud you in cold and darkness, yet each day you see your sun." I fancied a lily moved its yellow tongue and answered me—such is the trickery of love—saying: "When the sun that you adore, Inés, shines on you at night, when all other suns are spent, is not that a greater fortune?" . . .

TELLO: (*aside*) Thus did a Greek philosopher once answer a blind man who bemoaned his lot: "The night brings its own pleasures," so what has she to complain about?

INÉS: I come as a moth to a candle, longing for your light. . . . No, not as a moth, but as a phoenix, for in the flame of this passion, I burn and die, and then am born again.

ALONSO: Thrice blessed be the coral of these lips. The delicate petals of a rose whose scent in loving words gives me both life and strength. I, too, when Tello is not there to hear me, tell my love, my hopes, my fears, to the flowers.

TELLO: (*aside*) I've even seen him in Olmedo talking to the radishes. Lovers are all the same, they'll talk to the stones or the wind.

ALONSO: My thoughts cannot endure either to be alone or silent. They must be with you, sweet Inés. Oh, if I could only say now all that I say to you in your absence! But when I am with you, I forget even to live. As I ride here, Inés, I recount to Tello all your graces, all your charms, your wit, your understanding. The mere sound of your name is so sweet to me that I gave employment to a serving woman simply because she bore your name. In addressing her all day, I imagine that I speak to you.

TELLO: Madam, your power over us is so great that you have turned my master into a poet and made a musician of me. Here is a song he has composed in your honor.

(*He sings*)

> When Inés walked in the valley,
> The sky offered all its stars
> In exchange for the pale primroses
> That were gathered by hands like hers.
> As I walked alone in the valley,
> The dew fell in tears to see
> How I offered my heart with the flowers,
> But she scorned to pluck it from me.

> She gathered the flowers in the valley,
> But mocked the heart I gave.
> The only hands that will welcome it
> Are the pale hands of a grave.

INÉS: You belie me, Tello. I would not banish my lord's heart to the grave.

ALONSO: No, Inés, it is my love that is belied in the song, for no verses could ever convey such depths of meaning as lie in my love for you.[20]

The original of the poem, as Jill Booty notes, is a complex and highly stylized gloss (*glosa*) on a popular song which runs roughly as follows: "I left Inés / laughing down in the valley / If you should see her, Andrés, / tell her I am dying, / and hardly may rally." Each successive stanza in the Spanish culminates in one of these lines from the popular song.

Some of the baroque splendor of the verse comes over even in translation, showing the similarity of Lope's elaborate, complex embellishment to the euphuistic expressions of Shakespeare. (I use the adjective "euphuistic" here to mean "beautifully decorative and ornamental," not the harsh, biased meaning generally given by dictionaries as "affected, farfetched," etc.) Shakespeare without euphuism would not be the Shakespeare we know. Lope de Vega without gongorism, which he often ridiculed but allowed to influence him, would not be the Lope we know. Marinism in Italy, *preciosité* in France, euphuism in England, gongorism in Spain—each differed from the others, nationalistically—but each highlighted complex baroque adornment, affording a wealth of metaphor and simile which was utilized to the fullest to interpret and dramatize "the warring passions of feelings, memories, desires and other inhabitants of the mind."

Lope de Vega was an immense torrent of lyricism, with a lyrical prolificacy that stupefies. He had inherited the results of the revolution in Spanish poetry of the sixteenth century, brought about when Italian meters were adapted to Spanish verse. Lope as a youth preferred traditional Spanish meters for a while, but the use of a large variety of meters became widespread and he was a product of his times. So he employed every poetic form known whether from learned Renaissance or from popular Spanish ballads (in Spanish called *romances*).

Where is his poetry to be found? The answer is, throughout his plays (all of which were written in verse) and interspersed throughout all of his prose works, such as *La Arcadia, La Dorotea,* and so forth. In addition, he published collections of his poems which he himself selected from his plays and other works; two such volumes are *Human Rhymes* (*Rimas humanas,* 1602) and *Human and Divine Rhymes* (*Rimas humanas y divinas,* 1634).

Before Lope de Vega's time many plays were written in prose; the best-known playwright to use prose was Lope de Rueda (*ca.* 1510–65). But prose lost out to verse, and verse drama became the standard for many years to follow. Unlike the writers of French classical drama, who employed a single type of verse, the Alexandrine, the Spanish playwrights used a variety of forms. The Spanish poet felt that a sudden alteration of the protagonist's fortunes, or a quick change of tone from tragic to comic, required corresponding change of verse forms: for example, in *The Courageous Cordovan* (*El cordobés valeroso,* Act I, scene 16) the King of Granada changed from speaking in verse of four lines of eight syllables each (*redondillas*) to octaves (*octavas*) when he reacted with indignation to the denunciation of the Abencerrajes as traitors; or in *The Adversities of Stephanie* (*La desdichada Estefanía,* Act II, scene 3), when Castro is told that his beloved has married a rival, he immediately switches from *redondillas* to ballad (*romance*) verse in order to heighten the effect of his bitterness toward the lady. Lope's changing of verse pattern from one act to the next was the norm, as also was changing its pattern when he went from dialogue to monologue, or from king to hidalgo, or from hidalgo to *gracioso.*

Lope had great affection for the sonnet. It seemed to him to be the appropriate vessel for one concept, one single, striking idea succinctly expressed, with the possibility for a brilliant, telling conclusion. Let the sonnet on repentance translated by Longfellow (quoted at the end of Chapter I) suffice to indicate his mastery of this form. Until very late in his lifetime, he employed the sonnet for lyrical soliloquies, although he rarely used it for dialogue or for dramatic exposition or narration. The dominant theme for the sonnet in his drama was ill-starred love and jealousy until toward the end of his career, when he chose it to express happier love sentiments. It should be noted that although Lope declared in his *New Art of Play Writing* that "the sonnet is good for expressing the feeling of people who are waiting," he himself used it little for this purpose. In his *Rhymes* (*Rimas*) he used the sonnet form for expressing every thought or emotion that caught his interest, ranging from the comic and trivial to the most profound. And one ought not forget that several of the infamous poems which caused his banishment were pornographic sonnets.

Other prevailing forms of verse employed by Lope are listed in the back of the present volume, with comments on their prevalence in his plays based on a monograph by Diego Marín.[21] A host of Lope's ballads, dealing principally with pastoral and Moorish themes, appeared in the *General Ballad Collection* (*Romancero general*, Madrid, 1600).

LOPE, CHAUVINIST—100 PER CENT SPANISH-ISM (ESPAÑOLISMO). In the theater, and in other works—such as *Drake the Pirate* (*La Dragontea*, 1598) for example—Lope repeatedly exhibited a magniloquent chauvinism. Audiences in Spain, and undoubtedly those of the Spanish empire wherever Lope was popular, must have felt intense pride in what might be called "100 per cent Spanish-ism." As today nations often assume that their side and God's are identical in war, just so did the seventeenth-century Spaniard: God, Country, King (*Dios, Patria, Rey*). One package.

In *Spaniards in Flanders* (*Los españoles en Flandes*), Lope has a Flemish girl, Rosela, exclaim, "Spaniard! How sweet the name sounds!" He uses Rosela as his mouthpiece to exalt Spain and Spaniards. The Spaniard's bearing is uniquely impressive, easily recognized. He is genteel with women, courteous, manly, unafraid of any man of flesh and blood, and even of the principalities of evil. His king is superior to all other kings, and His Majesty's army strikes terror by the mere mention of its name abroad. Spaniards are great lovers. "When I see a Spaniard. . . . any Spaniard. . . . my heart follows him, and it seems that the very rays of the sun itself stream from him. And this particular Spaniard [with whom she is in love], God knows!, is a man of

[ 85 ]

such spirit, bubbling humor, and such a fine figure that I would prefer having him for my own to wearing the crown of the Empire. How gracefully he puts on his hat! With what a firm gait he walks!"

Of their love-making, she declares Spanish men have "such infallible discrimination that they know instinctively when to caress and when to cuff."

Here is a miscellany of Lope's encomiums: Spanish and traitor are incompatible terms. A Spaniard's word is his bond. His ingratiating personal qualities and his devoted attention to the ladies are learned from nursery days: "I am Spanish, and we Spaniards learn in the cradle to attend the ladies" ("Soy español, y el amparar las damas desde la cuna lo aprendemos"), declared a character in a play appropriately entitled *Spanish Courtesy* (*La cortesía de España*). One wonders if any other nation could boast of a playwright who could construct an entire play out of its national comity.

Nor was the formerly celebrated *furia española* overlooked by Lope. He repeatedly boasted about Spanish fury, and with a kind of picaresque chauvinism placed comments about it on the lips of characters from Tenerife, Turkey, the Island of Rhodes, the Canary Islands, and elsewhere. Lope even has the Grand Turk Suleiman the Magnificent declare that Spanish fury "blinds his senses." The Spaniard, in short, was the finest person in the world—noble, chivalrous, blessed with the world's best language, designed by nature to rule a world empire.

> Isn't the sun the brightest light in the sky?
> Then why should it distress you that the
> Spaniard is the best person on earth?
> Deny not his courtesy, language, nobility,
> government, laws. Why then
> should he not be ruler over all
> that the sun surveys and brings forth?
> —*The Valiant Céspedes* Act II

> La mejor luz en el cielo,
> ¿no es el sol? Pues si es el sol,
> ¿qué te causa desconsuelo
> que sea el hombre español
> el mejor hombre del suelo?

> Confesad su pulicia,
> su lenguaje, su hidalguía
> su república, sus leyes
> Pues, ¿por qué no han de ser reyes
> de cuanto el sol mira y cría?
> —*El valiente Céspedes,* Act II

A certain character named Chaves de Villalba put up this sign challenging all comers: "The King of Spain is the finest king on earth. The Spanish nobleman who makes this challenge will fight a duel to maintain this claim."

Another character, not a Spaniard, muttered after reading the challenge:

> That's a Spaniard for you! Who else?
> No one so daring as a Spaniard,
> No one so honorable as a Spaniard,
> No one so brave as a Spaniard,
> No one so successful in love as a Spaniard!
> What a courageous challenge!
> Who defends his country best? The Spaniard.
> Who defends his King best? The Spaniard.
> Who is the best warrior? The Spaniard.
> Who maintains the law? The Spaniard.
> The Spaniard has everything!
> Everybody wants to surpass the Spaniard,
> Everybody wants to see the Spaniard,
> Everybody looks at the Spaniard,
> envious of his power.
> —*The Blazon of the Chaves of Villalba,* Act I

¡Español hubo de ser . . . !
> Nadie tiene atrevimiento
> como español, nadie honor
> como español, nadie aliento
> como español, nadie amor
> como español. ¡Bravo intento!
> ¿Quién defiende bien su tierra?
> Español; ¿quién a su Rey?
> Español; ¿quién hace guerra?
> Español; ¿quién guarda ley?
> ¡Español todo lo encierra!

Todos desean vencer
al español; todos ver
al español; todos mirar
al español; porque admiran
la envidia de su poder.
—*El blasón de los Chaves de Villalba*, Act I

Characteristically when Lope put non-Spanish personages on the stage, he saw them through a Hispanic eyepiece. All places, all characters—Moorish, Christian, heretic, pagan, American Indian, Japanese, or whatever—are strained through his *españolismo*, his Spanishness. The upper classes—whether Russian, English, Saracen, Roman, or German—fit the image that Lope and his contemporaries had of Spanish upper classes, even to their sense of honor. Almost all Lopean characters looked, talked, acted, and reacted like seventeenth-century Spaniards.

Even though Lope protested in his *New Art of Play Writing* against the general apathy of producers toward faithful rendition of local color in the wardrobe department, he himself proved to be equally as apathetic in portraying non-Spaniards. He must have seen and met numbers of foreigners in a world capital such as Madrid was in its heyday. Yet he rigged out his foreigners inwardly and outwardly with Spanish characteristics. The following dialogue from *Make-Believe Becomes Truth* (*Lo fingido verdadero*) exhibits Lope's hispanization of ancient classic personages.[22] A player, Ginés, is "talking theater" with the Emperor Diocletian:

GINES: Would you like to see *Andria* by Terence?
DIOCLETIAN: That old stuff? Certainly not!
GINES: Then how about Plautus's *The Boastful Soldier*?
DIOCLETIAN: That's not much better. No—give me a brand new story rich in invention and spare me the arty stuff. My taste in plays is Spanish [*sic*]. If you give me realism, my attention wanders and I get bored . . .

Lope's works contain a host of foreigners. The Morley-Tyler statistics on nationalities portrayed by Lope reveal six pages of names of characters with Italian names, four pages of Moorish names, four of French, and so on.[23] Why, with foreigners abounding in his works, was he so unconcerned with making them authentic? A. A. Parker says the seventeenth-century Spanish dramatists followed the principle that drama is essentially a portrayal of action (plot) and not primarily of characterization. Characterization held a secondary place in their thinking because they felt (as did Aristotle) that a play should have action lavished with incident. In these circumstances little time was left to elaborate character, which was generally restricted to brief touches. The twentieth century, says Parker, with its characteristic "realistic" conception of drama (and life) is likely to misunderstand—and show its disapproval of—playwriting which does not place characterization to the fore.[24]

## HONOR, REPUTATION, AND FACE-SAVING—SEÑORAS AND SEÑORITAS ON PRECARIOUS PEDESTALS

> My dear dear lord,
> The purest treasure mortal times afford
> Is spotless reputation: that away,
> Men are but gilded loam or painted clay . . .
> Mine honor is my life; both grow in one;
> Take honor from me, and my life is done.
> —*King Richard the Second*, I, i,
> by William Shakespeare

It is a far cry from the seventeenth-century hidalgo's "Antes que todo es mi dama"—freely, "my lady first"—to the twentieth-century masculine code of conduct toward women. Golden-Age Spanish drama is full to the brim with honor—threatened, lost, or cruelly avenged.[25] Some have claimed that Spain's rules of honor reflected the actual daily conduct of Spaniards (James Fitzmaurice-Kelly, Ricardo del Arco y Garay), but Rudolph Schevill maintained that they were mostly convention.[26] My opinion is that some of the code of honor, termed *pundonor*, was conventional, much as is the code bravado of the stylized fictional cowboys of today, so reckless with six-shooter and life and limb. Some Europeans still think our Westerns are a mirror held up to American life. Many scholars believe Lope de Vega's theater was a like mirror.

Honor and a decent woman were inseparable. Well-born

women were kept in seclusion and allowed on the streets only if veiled and accompanied. The fashion of the veiled woman, or *tapada,* was so strong in sixteenth-century Spain that it crossed the Atlantic Ocean practically unchanged by the sea voyage, into colonial Spanish America, and survives today in the *tapada* motif for silver work and other artifacts in Peru.

Spanish women were thought to be weak creatures devoid of strong moral principle so that strict espionage and snooping on any and all of the affairs of a wife or unmarried sister were expected of the men. At the same time, women were placed on pedestals, something precious but fragile, forever compared to glass.

Honor was a metaphysical entity deposited, so to speak, in the valor of the man and in the fidelity of the woman. Sometimes the metaphysics of the "place of deposit" of honor seems fanciful, as for example, in *The Sheep Well* (*Fuenteovejuna*). In this play the father explains at some length the timing of the "transfer" of honor responsibility from himself and his son to his ravished daughter's new husband. The transfer of responsibility to the latter would come with the consummation of their marriage. Men and women in Lope's audience nodded approval and said, "This is the way things are" ("Con tal condición nacimos"). Lope said in his *New Art of Play Writing* that no theme surpassed honor in popularity in his day.

According to the formula "because I'm a woman and I need your help" ("por mujer y desdichada"), any lady could request and expect protection from any male in sight against any enemy or enemies; and under penalty of losing face no gentleman could deny her assistance.

In the custom of the day, if a lady were to offend a gentleman —with taunts, of course, since "fair feminine hands do not offend" ("Las manos blancas no ofenden")—he might not retaliate against her; instead, custom decreed he should challenge to a duel any gentleman who had witnessed the slight, called in Spanish *desaire.* Paradoxically, the challenge to the duel had to be offered only after the lady was out of sight and earshot, "for no man who is challenged in the presence of a lady need accept the challenge" ("Porque ningún hombre dió satisfacción que se pide delante de una mujer").

The code required further that the recipient of an affront receive satisfaction without attendant publicity because the insult to honor multiplied each time someone else learned of it. Again, paradoxically, if an affronted husband retaliated in secret and his secret was disclosed, the public applauded his action, no matter how sanguinary. A young contemporary of Lope, Calderón de la Barca, left the most notorious example of a husband's secret revenge in *The Doctor of His Own Honor* (*El médico de su honra*). The husband, don Gutierre Alfonso Solís, ordered a doctor to bleed his wife Mencía to death because her ex-suitor, Prince Henry, courted her (unsuccessfully) during Gutierre's absence. Gutierre knew that Mencía was innocent, but had her murdered to wash his honor clean.

In the same author's *Secret Vengeance for Secret Wrong* (*A secreto agravio, secreta venganza*), the husband invited the suspected lover of his wife on a boat trip, drowned him, then made it all appear to be accidental. Next he burned down his own house, with his wife inside, and made this too appear accidental: first water, then fire to wipe clean the abstract stain. The play was allegedly based on a true story. The then current phrase "con tal condición nacimos," spoken with a resigned nod of the head, expressed the unavoidability of violent "restoration" of lost honor. One feels, on reading a number of the honor plays, that the "laws" of honor were generally considered to be among the immutable laws of the universe. The king in the play entitled *El médico de su honra* thoroughly approved of the husband's revenge taken on an innocent wife, victim of unsound circumstantial evidence.

Generally Lope de Vega avoided the gory extremes of his younger contemporary, Calderón. But not always. In *The Knights-Commanders of Cordoba* (*Los comendadores de Córdoba*) Lope has the husband kill two suspected gentlemen, his wife, all their accomplices, *and* the domestic animals he meets en route to carry out his purpose. And in *Justice Without Revenge* (*El castigo sin venganza*), considered one of Lope's finest plays, he measures up to any Calderonian gory horror. In this play Casandra, daughter of the Duke of Mantua, is to be married to the Duke of Ferrara. Ferrara sends his illegitimate son, Federico, to receive her; en route to the Ferrara estate, in a stagecoach accident, Federico saves her from harm and carries her in his arms to safety. They fall in love instantly. As the play moves forward, everything in their experience seems to push them toward illicit consummation, not excepting the licentiousness of the Duke of Ferrara, who abandoned his bride the morning after his wedding night for sequent nights with Ferrara prostitutes. Later he marched off to war to fight for "God and the Pope," and the young people, now alone, can resist no longer. The Duke returns from battle profoundly reformed, determined henceforth to alter his conduct, become a new man and live like a saint. But when the blow of the knowledge of his secret dishonor strikes him, he abruptly returns to his old revengeful self, binds and gags Casandra, places her in a sack to conceal her identity from her lover and orders her slain by Federico. Federico carries out the hideous order, whereas the Duke immediately orders Federico executed "for the murder of his stepmother," claiming Federico's greedy motive was the fear of losing the inheritance of the dukedom to the unborn child of the pregnant Casandra. Three lives were snuffed out for the "honor" of a licentious man, and Lope once again shows how the foggy dominion of honor was cruelly governed by a bewildering profusion of mischievous paradoxes.

Lope, like his contemporaries, thoroughly condemned "the bestial cruelty" of the code of honor. He used the Duke of Ferrara as his spokesman:

They [Federico and Casandra] have confessed their guilt. Now, *honor*, you must be the judge and execute both the sentence and the punishment. For a man whose honor has been publicly avenged ever carries with him some trace of the foulness with which it was stained. No living soul must know that I have suffered this disgrace, and I must bury my dishonor as though it had never existed. Once the offense is known, nothing can erase it from the minds of men. . . . Honor, cruel enemy of mankind! Who was the first to impose your harsh law upon the world? Who first ordained that you should reside in women's keeping and not in men's? The worthiest man may lose you, though he commits no sin at all. A barbarous tyrant, and no man of discernment, invented this fierce stricture.

—*Justice Without Revenge*, Act III

A sovereign could do no wrong, yet paradoxically he could dishonor a lady if he paid court to her (even if in vain) and word leaked out. By his action he stained the reputation of all the male members of her family. The method for removing the stain was to remove the lady from this life, never to bring reprisals on the sacred person of the king.

Dueling in Lope's day implied equality of social standing. One could not fight with an inferior except incognito.

The clan spirit was dominant. Any smudge on the honor of one member of the family stained all, even cousins. Men might "restore" honor in one of four ways: (1) an apology by one of the contending parties, which required guts; (2) a duel; (3) a marriage; (4) taking the life of the one on the distaff side who was under a cloud. If two gentlemen were dueling and news was brought them that two of their relatives had just married, the duel was called off and no disgrace was involved for either.

Next to the claims of family and Eros were those of friendship. Unless love intervened and took precedence, one owed perfect loyalty to a friend—to cherish his honor exactly as one's own. This obligation was summed up in a proverb, "Comradeship above all else" (*Con quien vengo vengo*). In contradiction to this was the phrase, "In what concerns me, I come first" (*Primero soy yo*). Yet as if these last two honor maxims were still not sufficiently paralogistic, there was still another rule requiring honor itself to yield where necessary to a lady's welfare: "My lady first" (*Antes que todo es mi dama*).

Logic-chopping was frequent. Hairsplitting subtleties arose. If one encountered two duelists fighting and each was one's friend, one faced an enigma; so first he attempted to adjust their differences. If he failed, he assisted the *challenged* friend. If the occasion arose, a gentleman would abandon either a friend or a kinsman to answer the superior claims on his sword-arm of his sovereign or the lady of his affections. The honor code of the seventeenth century was a sort of glottological Kingdom of Okeefenokee with Contradiction as its anointed tyrant.

Concerning the depths of the roots of the Spanish honor code, Ramón Menéndez Pidal, in *The Spaniards in Their History*,[27] says he found incontestable proof in medieval Spanish literature that Spaniards exalted passion for honor in the Middle Ages fully equal to Calderón's in the seventeenth century. Américo Castro attempts to explain why honor has played such a dominant role in Spanish life and literature.[28] And Alfonso García Valdecasas calls the rebirth of a new and "unfalsified" sense of honor (he doesn't quite spell it out) among men today a *sine qua non* for the survival of the human race.[29]

Yet for good or evil, the pendulum has swung, and much of Spain's drama of the seventeenth century invites apathy mainly because of radically changed attitudes toward sex. Twentieth-century audiences have little patience with the *pundonor* as a dramatic motive. Our current attitudes are reflected in the following catchwords culled from recent miscellaneous American sources: jealousy is infantile frustration; the double standard is a capitalistic exploitation of women; love, instead of being the fountainhead of every noble action, is a sign of sick psyche; love is the biological urge of Nature to preserve the race; constancy in love is a neurotic fixation; singing love-songs is a regressive tendency toward immature labial pleasures; virginity is an old-fashioned something left on the back seat of a parked car; fornication is nothing more than liberalism in sex attitudes.

Yet the Spaniard in Lope's day wrapped up in this one single package of *pundonor* such fundamental aspects of his emotional life as sex, reputation, face-saving, patriotism (monarchical style), and the jeopardy of both temporal and eternal welfare (in a duel he might die unrepentant).

Both civil and religious authorities condemned dueling, but in vain. On the stage a hidalgo without a sword would have felt improperly dressed, and men with honor in their souls and swords by their sides offered the perfect device for instant conflict—and conflict is called the *sine qua non* of successful drama.

III *Humor High and Low:* The Gracioso and the
Hidalgo—The Four Esses: Suspense, Surprise,
Sensation, Shock

Lope de Vega drew his humorous characters from several social levels, but most often he mined the lower classes for his principal comic staple, his clowns, or *graciosos*. They constituted the surest, easiest laugh-getters, and he was warily mindful that laughter was so highly treasured that it assured success at the box office of plays which, minus humor, might otherwise fail.

He was always too low on cash to risk being stoic about the financial losses of a flop.

The *graciosos* embraced nearly every conceivable quality: shrewdness, wit, ingeniousness in inventing tricks and deceits, resourcefulness in volunteering solutions to problems and surmounting all manner of obstacles. They were full of folk saws, apothegms, moral tales, proverbs, and ready information, and not infrequently substantial classical learning. They could be and often were loyal, devoted and self-sacrificing friends. They might be either sex, but were most often male. Some were skillful folk singers.

Loyal *graciosos* aroused pity and pathos, somewhat like King Lear's jester. But they could be, and frequently were, frightened turncoats easily intimidated. The same is true, although to a lesser degree, of the female comedian, the *graciosa,* who attended the heroine. Perhaps in their brilliance of mental traits lay their chief lack of realism, for too often they represented the perennial resourcefulness of Lope's own comic gifts which were considerably beyond the *vis cómica* of servants.

The *graciosos* were nearly always servants, living in, and hence Lope could easily march them on and off the stage more or less logically—a much-coveted setup for any playwright. They invariably accompanied the protagonist, often as a foil, so that even when a scene was "de camino" (on the highway), the playwright could easily manage their entrances and exits. They repeatedly parodied the principals by comically duplicating their actions or by rowdily burlesquing their words and attitudes toward honor, courtship, love, valor, or any subject whatsoever, however sacred. They even parodied passionate Petrarchian love verses, often providing "instant laughter" by turning very high moments of breath-taking pathos into merriment in a split second; the swineherd Pelayo provides an example in *The King the Greatest Alcalde.* Don Tello, the petty feudal tyrant of this *comedia,* had stolen Sancho's bride Elvira at the altar, and Sancho must travel a great distance to ask the king to force Tello to return her. Pelayo accompanies him. On the heels of a breath-taking lyrical apostrophe of leave-taking addressed to Elvira by Sancho, Pelayo took leave of his pigs.

NUÑO [Elvira's father]: Adiós, Sancho.
SANCHO [Elvira's fiancé]: Adiós, Elvira.
PELAYO: Adiós, puercos. [Adieu, my lovely little porkers.]

With Lope, when the opportunity to make an audience laugh appears, anything goes. He was an unruly genius. He wrote a movingly tragic scene for the ending of *Diana Kidnapped* (*El robo de Diana*), then mutilated the tender mood just created by bringing on a clown smeared with flour. One could wish Lope had more frequently given us more continuity of thought uninterrupted by slapstick. In *Saint Pedro Nolasco*, Act I, a friar-*gracioso*, Pierres, arrives with money to ransom the saint from the Moors, when a fiery Moorish girl, Alifá, because Pierres is the instrument for taking away the man she loves (Saint Pedro Nolasco), has him flogged and tossed out, mainly for laughs. The taste of the public was for religion not unmixed with humor. Lope catered to it.

Then as now in Spain, laughter was eagerly sought by the populace and gladly paid for at the box office. In Lope's time audiences seemed disappointed if any play lacked its comedian. It was in this environment that Lope developed the *gracioso* from the mere simpleton of his predecessors into the more complex *gracioso* who was soon appearing in almost all Spanish plays, including the solemn and religious *auto sacramental* (one-act Eucharistic play).

By no means were all of his *graciosos* clodpates like Pelayo. Some of his most memorable characters were comic. In *Justice Without Revenge* (*El castigo sin venganza*), the buffoon Batín resembles King Lear's jester. Batín, at least until near the play's end, acts as loyal companion of the young protagonist, Prince Federico. Another *gracioso*, Alano, in *Mirror for the Nobility* (*Los nobles cómo han de ser*), is an astute but caustic critic of society who appears in one scene with a flycatcher for use on unpalatable human types; he paints us a satirical picture of seventeenth-century anti-social characters by reciting (in rhyme, of course) who they were and what were their most palpable shortcomings.

In Tello, the *gracioso* of *St. John's Night* (*La noche de San Juan*), Lope portrays a gadfly to poets; and in Chacón, the comic of *The Stunning Beauty* (*La niña de plata*), Lope creates a hilarious poet-baiter who admits (Act III) to being four times a poet and . . . "The first time I got out of it with a flogging; the second time four priests exorcised me; the third time people forced me off the street 'for being diseased'; and the fourth time, by Heaven, I won a pair of gloves with a sonnet, and just listen to it:"

> Violante commands me to write a sonnet,
> and I've never been so pressed in my life.
> They say a sonnet contains fourteen lines;
> Oddly already I've written three lines just above this one.
> I thought I'd never find a rhyme,
> Yet here I am in the middle of the first quatrain;
> Now then, if I ever reach the first tercet
> nothing in this quatrain will faze me.
> Well, here I go into the first tercet,
> and I seem to have stepped in on my right foot,
> since with this verse go its finishing touches.
> Now I'm in the second tercet, and I even suspect
> I'm finishing up thirteen lines already;
> Count and see if there aren't fourteen—and I'm done.

> (Un soneto me manda hacer Violante,
> y en mi vida me he visto en tanto aprieto.
> Catorce versos dicen que es soneto;
> burla burlando van los tres delante.
> Yo pensé que no hallara consonante,
> y estoy a la mitad de otro cuarteto;
> mas si me veo en el primer terceto,
> no hay cosa en los cuartetos que me espante.
> Por el primer terceto voy entrando,
> y parece que entré con pie derecho,
> pues fin con este verso le voy dando.
> Ya estoy en el segundo, y aun sospecho
> que voy los trece versos acabando;
> contad si son catorce, y está hecho.)[30]

The constant impecuniosity of Lope's *graciosos* made most of them venal: one of them, Tello, in *The Eighth Wonder* (*La octava maravilla*), even claimed inheritance of his venality, so to speak, through his genes; of his father he said: "Before he died, my old man ordered one hand be left sticking out of his grave, just in case somebody offered him something."

Since hunger and threadbare clothes accompanied poverty, the *graciosos* almost invariably preferred food-and-clothes-talk to the love-talk of their masters. The ragged and hungry in the audience naturally responded to this poor-mouth chatter because they inhabited an ill-fed Spain, bankrupt in spite of the flow of money from her far-flung colonies.

Lope de Vega created many Pelayos, Batines, Brunos, Tirsos, and other *graciosos*. He assigned to the great majority of them similar fundamental characteristics,[31] whether he made them lackeys, peasants, clodhoppers, or even sextons, such as Corrizo in *The Good Custodian* (*La buena guarda*). Corrizo, the friar-sacristan of this latter play based on an old legend, is a scold with a sarcastic tongue for laymen who deviate from his ideas of strict conduct—until he, too, is "corrupted" by the music and festivities of some mysterious villagers who awaken his dormant desires for pleasure. The main plot follows the familiar story of the erring nun who broke her vows to run off with her lover, but returned repentant, although unmissed, because an angel had substituted for her. Of special comic interest here is the *second* angelical substitute for the comic Corrizo, who had simultaneously deserted his post also.

Among the great variety of types Lope lifted from the masses was the buffoon, or king's jester, in Spanish called *pieza de Rey*. These clowns enjoyed unchecked license even in the lofty atmosphere of the royal palace. "To think," said a character in *Don Luis de Almansa's Javelin* (*Lanza por lanza, la de don Luis de Almansa*), "that these fools enter brashly, stopped by nobody, when we are left here to wait in the portal like a pair of sculptured savages." The license of these buffoons was so broad that they heaped on scoffing with a heavier hand than the *graciosos*.

Occasionally a jester, such as Lirano in *The Ring of Forgetfulness* (*La sortija del olvido*), was both musician and poet and more sympathetic than his numerous licentious colleagues. He had a keen understanding of his trade: ". . . yo, y cuantos graciosos hoy vivimos andamos por sacarle a quien decimos las gracias y donaires que sabemos, que es la renta y oficio que tenemos,"—which summarized means that jokes and wit were his and his colleagues' craft and livelihood, their stock-in-trade. Although the buffoon was a "common man," he bewailed his condition with dignified speech. Lope's remind us of the pathetic clowns painted by Velázquez.

Perhaps those from a small-town childhood can recall a town half-wit who supplied merriment, generally ribald, to the rough-necks and idlers who gathered in stores and barber shops on Saturday nights. Among the comic characters in Lope's reper-tory the most sensational, if also the most pathetic, were some-times just such half-wits. Their names became common currency in the satires, plays, and ballads of the day, and some of their names survive today in literature: Raw Chicken (Pollo Crudo), Olive-oil Lamp (Candil), and don Pascual de la Corte Binorre, for example.

One of Lope's plays is named outright *The College Half-Wit* (*El bobo del colegio*); in it a young Lothario-protagonist stoops to conquer by pretending temporarily to be a *bobo* in order to obtain a half-wit's special privileges in his beloved's hometown. His stooping went along well with his lady love—and with Lope's audience.

As a contrast with the "low humor" of the *graciosos*, Lope de Vega also wrote numberless scenes of sophisticated humor which grew out of the plot and characterization of the hidalgo protago-nists, especially women. In *Silly in Public, Discreet in Private* (*La boba para los otros y discreta para sí*) for example, Lope features a simple country girl named Diana. She was unaware of being the daughter of a duke until she was called to her father's dukedom to fill the high position of authority made vacant by his death; immediately she was surrounded by in-triguing enemies, but triumphed over them by always affecting a naïve simplicity in public. In private Diana managed her peo-ple's interests with unusual perspicacity, and carried on a love intrigue with a nobleman, whom she married. The wit she con-cealed under her feigned naïveté gave rise to the humor of the play, and the playwright maintained a gay atmosphere through-out all three acts.

Lope created numerous women characters quite as charming and gay as this Diana. One of his most fascinating is Belisa in

*The Iron Tonic of Madrid* (*El acero de Madrid*). Lisardo, the
hero, accompanied by his friend Riselo, appears watching anx-
iously at the door of a fashionable church in Madrid. He hopes
to see a lady (Belisa) at the conclusion of the service. At this
moment Belisa appears attended by her nagging aunt Theodora,
whose windy piety seems outwardly exaggerated by the style
of her dress, inspired obviously by religiosity, not religion.

THEODORA: Show more of gentleness and modesty;
  Of gentleness in walking quietly,
  Of modesty in looking only down
  Upon the earth you tread.
BELISA: That is just what I am doing.
THEODORA: What? When you're looking straight at that young man?
BELISA: Did you not bid me look upon the earth?
  And what is he but just a bit of it?
THEODORA: I said the earth whereon you tread, niece.
BELISA: But that whereon I tread is hidden quite
  With my own petticoat.
THEODORA: Words such as these become no well-bred maid, Belisa.
  But, by your mother's blessed memory,
  I'll put an end to all your tricks.
  What! You look back at him again?
BELISA: Who, me?
THEODORA: Yes, you—and made him secret signs besides.
BELISA: I did not. It's only that you troubled me
  With nagging questions and vexatious replies,
  So that I stumbled and looked round to see
  Who would prevent me from falling.
RISELO: (*To Lisardo*). She falls again;
  Be quick and help her.
LISARDO: (*To Belisa*). Pardon me, lady,
  And forgive my glove.
THEODORA: Whoever saw the like!
BELISA: Thank you, sir; you saved me from a fall.
LISARDO: An angel, lady, might have fallen so,
  or stars that shine with heaven's own blessed light.
THEODORA: I can fall, too, but not for your tricks, sir. Go now. Leave
  us.
LISARDO: Your servant, Madam. (*Aside as he withdraws*) Heaven
  deliver me from such an old scold.

THEODORA: (*To Belisa*) A pretty fall you made of it; and now, I
    hope, you'll be satisfied, since he assisted you.
BELISA: And you no less satisfied, since now you'll have a reason to
    plague me for a solid week.
THEODORA: But why again do you turn your head?
BELISA: Why, sure you'd think it is wise
    To notice well the place I stumbled at,
    Lest I should stumble there when next I pass.
THEODORA: Fiddlesticks! I know your tricks.
    You'll not deny this time you looked straight at that young man
    again!
BELISA: Deny it? No!
THEODORA: You dare confess it then?
BELISA: I do. You saw him help me.
    And would you have me fail to thank him for it?
THEODORA: Oh! Let's go home, let's go home.
BELISA: Now we shall have enough scolding cooked up out of this
    to last a week. [Translated by George Ticknor; slightly modified.]

Spaniards have held merriment in high regard through the
centuries. One manifestation of this feeling is indicated by the
Spanish idiom *tener gracia*. *Gracia* means charm, elegance, harmony, favor; *tener gracia* means "to be funny." Lope de Vega's
*comedias* are peopled with young men and women who possess
the estimable characteristics suggested by the idiom *tener gracia*,
although the female is almost always superior to the male. The
male hidalgos amuse cleverly with banter and repartee, but they
rarely equal the women characters in spontaneous, unstrained,
and humorously mischievous vivacity.

THE FOUR ESSES—SURPRISE, SUSPENSE, SENSATIONALISM, SHOCK.
Lope de Vega combined ghosts and the supernatural with violence and the grotesque to heighten suspense and to bear his
audience in imagination as far as possible away from their drab
daily lives. In *The Jewish Girl from Toledo* (*La judía de Toledo*)
Lope not only has a messenger come from God (twice) to warn
King Alfonso to terminate his liaison with the beautiful Raquel,
but he also has the pair go on a fishing trip together and by way
of warning has the King snag the head of a dead child. In *The
Virgins of Simancas* (*Las doncellas de Simancas*) the Moors an-

nually exact a tribute of one hundred beautiful Christian virgins. The Christians for years were unable to develop enough courage and stamina to stop the tribute, until the year that one hundred virgins, led by a spirited girl named Leonor, mangled their own beauty by *cutting off their left hands* in order to become undesirable to their dark captors. This heroic, though grotesque, act sparked the men to try once again; they fought and won and stopped forever the hideous annual tribute.

In *Deserving of a Crown* (*La corona merecida*), the faithful doña Sol, a married woman after whom the King lusted, escaped being ravished by literally covering her body with cuts and wounds. In *The Duke of Viseo* (*El duque de Viseo*) Lope shocked his audience by showing a prepared "revelation," in the back-stage niche, of the body of the deceased duke on the throne *crowned,* his scepter at his feet, and the body of a lady (doña Elvira) there also, dead of a broken heart for love of him. In the course of the power struggle that developed in *The Assassinated Prince* (*El príncipe despeñado*), Lope paced through enough action and sensationalism for several plays: prophecy of divine justice; a child born in the wild woods; a beautiful lady ravished by King Sancho; the lady's house draped in black; the lady taking her own life; the prince thrown from a cliff.

In *The Reluctant Bride and Groom from Hornachuelos* (*Los novios de Hornachuelos* (of disputed authorship) the playwright put in a kind of nonviolent grotesquerie by portraying King Henry III so reduced to penury that he had to barter an article of clothing for his supper, yet seeming nevertheless so regal in his bearing that he caused considerable turbulence in a subject by a mere glance. A king looked like a king, even in destitution.

*The Outrageous Saint* (*La fianza satisfecha*), with its existentialist hero, is a monstrous, brutal shocker, the equivalent of Shakespeare's *Titus Andronicus* in nearly every detail. Just as harsh to the sensibilities is a hideous incident in *The Ethiopian Prodigy* (*El prodigio de Etiopía*): a white heroine, who in Act I promises her hand to a Negro suitor, keeps her promise in Act III when she returns to the stage after a brief exit and (her eyes blazing with scorn) offers him her *severed* hand.

Although the Spaniards' ancient religio-political struggle with the invading Moors had become, by Lope's time, mostly memory, this national memory remained sharply and clearly delineated in the nation's folk songs and ballads. (The remaining *moriscos*—baptized Moors—were expelled early in the seventeenth century.) Lope capitalized on the nationalistic emotion arising from this collective memory of infidels, in which he no doubt shared. In *The Siege of Santa Fe* (*El cerco de Santa Fe*) he presented the ever popular Catholic monarchs, Ferdinand and Isabella, thrilling the public not only by their presence on stage, but also with some sensational love interest. The major characters of *The Siege of Santa Fe* hold to one of two warring religious faiths, Christian or Mohammedan. For a shocker, a Moor promised to bring back to his sweetheart three Christian heads after the impending battle against Ferdinand and Isabella's army. On the Christian side, a national Spanish hero, Fernán Pérez del Pulger, entered the Moorish-occupied city of Granada and there pinned an *Ave María* on the wall of a Mohammedan mosque. Sacrilegious insults issued from the mouths of characters on both sides. At the play's end, the Moors came out bested, naturally, in the war of words as well as in the war of swords. Sensationalism, suspense, violence, the triumph of Christian over Moor—all this was sure-fire at the box office.

Lope de Vega is a master of rapid exposition. He quickly acquaints his audience with essential details of the play's situation and theme, then moves rapidly forward, weaving in and out of action and counteraction, subplot, cross-purposes. "The usual analysis of Lope's characters fails to lay stress on the fact that, in rapidity of action, impulses must dominate over reason and deliberation because the latter demand too many delays to fit into his formula. . . . Careful scrutiny of the majority of Lope's plays reveals that he had no fixed conception of dramatic steps purely by acts and scenes, and only a sense of forward movement . . ."[32]

Good examples of Lope's rapid exposition are found in *The Reward for Honest Speech* (*Premio del bien hablar*), *Master Lucas* (*El dómine Lucas*), *Belisa's Pruderies* (*Los melindres de Belisa*), and *Sheepwell* (*Fuente Ovejuna*). *Rome in Ashes* (*Roma abrasada*) affords a specimen of a forward-moving action-packed play although it contains enough material for several plays. The play covers a twenty-year period in three brief acts.

Its incredible content includes the assassination of Emperor Claudius by Nero and Agrippina, Nero's love for Eta, Nero's murder of his mother (she was put to death and exposed in the niche of the stage in the usual "exposure" scene), a brief Old Testament-based account of world history, an episode of chauvinistic praise of Spain spoken by the "Spaniard," Seneca; the death of Seneca and Lucan; the plot to overthrow Nero; Nero's downfall and death; and a climactic burning of Rome. Almost any one of these incidents would supply material for a play built with fewer disproportions. But one cannot deny there is action.

Another heavily cluttered and ill-proportioned play is *The New World Discovered by Columbus* (*El nuevo mundo descubierto por Cristóbal Colón*). Here Lope attempted to present too many episodes in the life of the Admiral, in too many places: Barcelona, Granada, Portugal, on shipboard crossing the Atlantic (a mutiny occurs), and the West Indies. And he portrayed unconvincing Indians never seen on land or sea. Yet he gave his audience fast-moving action, packaged with religion, danger, and chauvinism.

In highlighting Lope's use and abuse of action at the expense of characterization, I am bound to say he wrote some notable exceptions. Such an exception is *Planting in Good Soil* (*El sembrar en buena tierra*), edited with care and acumen by William Fichter.[33] In Félix, the male protagonist, Lope created a superb character of a type of giddy youth that would be difficult to improve upon. It is thought that he wrote this *comedia* while under the influence of the beautiful but harum-scarum actress, Lucía de Salcedo, *la loca*, and that he drew the male protagonist right out of his own current personal follies. If this be true, he once again kept open a "hot line" from his heart to his pen, but this time minimizing abuse of action.

# CHAPTER 4

# Lope's Non-dramatic Works

## I Prose

LA ARCADIA, 1598. A rich though now abandoned mine of animal-, plant-, mineral-, and love-lore, a treasure of some of Lope's cleverest verse, La Arcadia[1] nevertheless is today, except for the interspersed verse, quite unreadable. It is a museum piece left over from the European appetite for the pastoral novel— once of gluttonous proportions—as witness Sannazaro's La Arcadia (1502), Jorge de Montemayor's frequently reprinted Diana (1559?), Cervantes' Galatea (1585), Sir Philip Sidney's Arcadia (1590), Honoré d'Urfé's L'Astrée (1607), and others.

The original Arcadia was a plateau in Greece, idealized and conventionalized by authors of pastoral literature into a land of jealous, loquacious, love-sick shepherds and shepherdesses. And it was common practice to conceal the identity of distinguished personages under a thin pseudonymy in this never-never land of fanciful sheep herders; authors and readers alike accepted the shepherd convention, not for a moment considering the characters to be unbathed rustics. In La Arcadia, for example, Lope uses such phraseology as "judicious shepherds" (discretos pastores) and even "learned shepherds" (doctos pastores).

Lope's use of pseudonymy afforded the added piquancy of a guessing game because distinguishing one conventionalized shepherd (i.e., celebrity) from another was an uncertain, hence tantalizing, business. One confuses Galafrón with Leriano, Anfriso with Alcino, even though Lope called his Arcadia "a true story," and declared that the incidents narrated were taken from life. He wrote La Arcadia at the request of the Duke of Alba. In it Lope called himself Belardo, the poetic name he used so frequently throughout his life. Following the usual pattern of pastoral novels, he interspersed verse with prose, constructing his plot along conventional pastoral lines.

Anfriso, "the most noble, virtuous, gallant, intelligent, brave and generous youth in Arcadia," said to be the nephew of Jupiter, is in love with Belisarda, "as beautiful as she is ill-starred." Anfriso's rival, the wealthy clodpate Salicio, favored by Belisarda's parents, "is as rich as he is ignorant, as presumptuous as he is rich, and as impudent as he is vulgar. . . ." Anfriso's parents separate him from Belisarda in the hope that he will forget her. He makes the acquaintance of a sorcerer who causes him to believe that Belisarda has been unfaithful. Suspicion and jealousy (probingly, baroquely, and lengthily analyzed by Lope) grip him, so that he turns to Anarda for solace. Word of his apparent desertion corrodes Belisarda's steadfastness, causing her to accept the suit of Salicio.

Next follows the tale of the giant, Alasto, inconveniently enamored of a normal-sized human nymph, Crisalda. In the midst of this intrigue comes the *tour de force* of naming a witches' brew of folklore from the animal and vegetable kingdoms.

Jealousy lurks behind every bush in Lope's *Arcadia*. Book Two provides a typical sample: there he personifies it as a beast, laments its ugliness and cruelty in highly ornamental rococo:

Jealousy is a hideous brute in the province of Suspicion, fleeter than an arrow; its sire is Love, its mother, Envy; it stole its eyes from Ire, its craving from the blind, its faith and language from the Greeks, its tongue from Deceit. Jealousy is as black as a crow, has the sight of a dragon, the illusions of an alchemist, the head of a stag [symbolically insinuating cuckoldry], the disposition of a lion when it suspects [its mate of] adultery, as many eyes as Juno placed on the tail of a peacock. It treads as lightly as a spy, sleeps as lightly as a sentinel, and its thoughts go wherever its imagination bids. It fears what it cannot see because its mistrust equates the excess of its punctilio. It goes about muffled at night, eavesdropping, and in the daytime appears as jaded as a man challenged to a duel. It stumbles along gropingly like a blind man, asking a thousand questions, moaning and making movements like those of a woman in childbirth. It eagerly treads into danger of death. It is an overthrown government in which blind Love wishes to destroy his own good name for reasons of state. Whoever named this beast Jealousy? Its name might better be *Hell*.

Today one leaves the reading of *La Arcadia* with the sensation a diamond miner must feel when he moves much earth to find only a tiny jewel now and then; in Lope's day the reader felt otherwise. The book went through fifteen editions in his lifetime, and many more later in the seventeenth century.[2]

The work is so riddled with classical references that one can hardly read a page without a dictionary of mythology at hand.

THE SHEPHERDS OF BETHLEHEM, *1612.* Lope de Vega dedicated *The Shepherds of Bethlehem* (*Los pastores de Belén*) to his young son Carlos Félix. It is a pastoral novel *a lo divino;* that is, the characters are shepherds resembling those of the pastoral novels, whereas the main drama concerns the birth of a divine being. It contains a variety of folklore, a literary contest, a child's game of forfeits, exquisite poetry, one of the tenderest cradle songs in the Spanish language, Bible lessons about David and Bathsheba, Absalom and Tamar, the question of Mary's ancestry, the love story of Amminadab, and even a *gracioso* called, humorously, Country Boy (Rústico). The work is held together by a plot setting forth activities of shepherds gathered in a valley near Bethlehem some weeks before the birth of Jesus. The tenderness and sincerity of the author's feelings toward Mary may be seen in the following description of the birth of Jesus:

When the Virgin sensed the moment of the birth of her beloved child, Joseph went outside because it did not appear seemly for him to witness such a holy sacrament. Then Mary removed the sandals from her blessed feet, took off her white mantle and the veil from her head, keeping on only the tunic; with her long and beautiful tresses of hair down over her shoulders, she laid out two cloths of linen and two of the finest quality of wool brought for the occasion and immaculately clean, and two smaller pieces to bind the divine head of her Son. . . . When she had all things in readiness, she knelt down and prayed, her back to the manger and her face raised on high, looking toward the east. . . . As she prayed she felt the movements of her Sovereign Son in her virginal womb, and in the twinkling of an eye he was born and she looked on him with her chaste eyes. . . . There lay upon the ground the glorious little creature, clean and white as snowflakes on the mountain—as white lilies nestled in their green leaves. . . . Then the Infant, crying out and shivering because of the cold and the hard ground, extended his feet and hands seeking the warmth and protection of his mother, who took him in her arms and held him against her breast; placing her face against his, she warmed and sheltered him with ineffable joy and maternal compassion. Then she held him in her virgin lap and began to wrap him carefully, blissfully, first in the two linen cloths, then in the wool; then with a sash she gently bound the precious little body; her strong arms picked up the one born to redeem the world; she bound His sovereign head for better protection, and when she had finished these pious signs of her maternal love, Joseph the blessed joined them again.

Similar tender passages are found throughout the book, which had considerable success, going through at least eight editions in the seventeenth century alone. However, printings after the first edition were bowdlerized by the Inquisition, which detected, or thought it detected, signs of excessive eroticism in certain passages. The Holy Office removed, for example, the story of Susanna and the Elders, and Absalom and Tamar, and other "erotic" episodes as well.

THE PILGRIM IN HIS OWN HOMELAND, *1604. The Pilgrim in His Own Homeland (El peregrino en su patria)*,[3] printed in Seville, is a complicated novel made up of stories of love and adventure, travel, hardships, shipwrecks, violence, jealousy, thieves, chance encounters (such as Pánfilo's accidental discovery of the wounded knight, in Book Four), and concluding with the final reunion of all the characters of the novel, with happiness and joy for everyone unconvincingly contrived. (The protagonists, Pánfilo de Luján and the beautiful Nise, experienced numerous hardships before being finally united in marriage.) Evidently the novel pleased in its day, for it went through six editions before 1618, and by 1621 had been translated anonymously into English as *The Pilgrim of Casteele,* and sold by one Thomas Dewe in St. Dunstaines Churchyard in Fleet Street in London.

Lope's model for the story was the Milesian tale and also Jerónimo de Contreras' *Jungle of Adventures (Selva de aventuras).* In the latter, the hero suffers a long series of calamities in foreign lands, whereas Lope has his hero suffer mainly in Spain: in Barcelona, Valencia, Zaragoza, and Toledo. Rage and cruelty alternate with tenderness and rapture. The hero is in turn courtier, soldier, captive, pilgrim, prisoner, madman, shepherd, and finally even a lackey in the household of those who caused his misadventures in the beginning. Lope interpolates some autobiography, as was his practice frequently—specifically his relationship with Micaela de Luján. He also intersperses lyric poems, from which come two of his most quotable observations: "For no *natural* conduct do we deserve either praise or censure" (Book One—referring to a youth's conduct in love); and "This short tyranny, this bait of youth, this illusion of sight, this prison of the soul, this darkener of the senses, which is called *Beauty*, and which heaven seems to give to women for our mischief" (Book Two).

Included in the volume with *The Pilgrim in His Own Homeland* (*El peregrino en su patria*) were four Eucharistic plays entitled *The Voyage of the Soul* (*El viaje del alma*), *The Wedding of the Soul and Divine Love* (*Las bodas del alma y del amor divino*), *Maya* (*La Maya*), and *The Prodigal Son* (*El hijo pródigo*), as well as the titles of 219 plays he listed as his. Lope said he prepared this list because of chagrin at the number of plays falsely published under his name and hawked throughout Spain and abroad. Although in listing plays authentically his, Lope was trying to claim what was his own, and disclaim what was not, before the ink was dry on his complaint and disclaimer, he said "confidentially" to foreigners who might read him that in Spain no one, including himself, wrote according to the precepts of dramatic art. If a playwright should attempt to do so, he said, his plays would not be tolerated by Spanish audiences. Here once again Lope is ambivalent toward his drama, like a father with a wayward son toward whom he is alternately affectionate and stern.

LA DOROTEA, *1632. La Dorotea*[4] is a novel told in dialogue form in five acts, interspersed with lyrical poems, each act concluding with a brief chorus. It is in places sentimental and romantic and as openly barefaced as the *Confessions* of Jean Jacques Rousseau. In fact, an alternate title could well be *Confessions* of Lope de Vega, if it weren't for the elaborate use of pseudonymy. He shares with his readers the story of the extravagances, wild ideas, inconstancies, caprices, whims, and even meannesses, infidelities, and deceits of his intemperate youth, and all in the name of a deathless but debasing sexual passion.

In *La Dorotea* Lope intermingles people with an allegorical character, Fame, and five allegorical choruses. The cast reads as follows, the principals indicated by asterisks: *Dorotea, a lady; * Teodora, her mother; * Gerarda, her friend; * Don Fernando, a gentleman; Julio, his tutor; Celia, maid to Dorotea; Felipa, daughter of Gerarda; César, astrologer; Ludovico, friend of César's and Don Fernando's; *Don Bela, Fernando's rival for Dorotea's favors; Laurencio, Don Bela's servant; * Marfisa, a lady; Clara, maid; Fame; Chorus on Love; Chorus on Power of Money; Chorus on Jealousy; Chorus on Vengeance; Chorus on Morality.

The plot concerns the loves of a bright young woman, Dorotea (really Elena Osorio), beautiful, refined, and educated, whose husband had gone to the New World not to return for five years. She has been the inamorata of the young poet and student, don Fernando (Lope). Fernando is poor, Dorotea's tastes are expensive; so after putting up ineffectual resistance, she gives in to the persistent entreaties of her mother, Teodora, and Gerarda, a Celestina, and plunges into a life of duplicity by accepting the advances (and the gold) of a wealthy suitor named Don Bela, called an *indiano* because of extended residence in the Spanish colonies. (*Indiano* was synonymous with "wealthy." The real-life pattern for Don Bela was an important person socially, the nephew of Cardinal Granvela.)

On learning of Dorotea's infidelity, Fernando is beside himself with jealousy. Hoping a change of scenery will bring solace, he obtains travel money by fraudulent means from another inamorata, Marfisa, and goes to Seville. Dorotea learns that Fernando has gone away and unsuccessfully attempts suicide by swallowing a diamond ring. Her method was in common usage among suicides although it ordinarily involved swallowing chipped diamonds. However, Lope, ever the dramatist, requires Dorotea to swallow a diamond whole.

Distance increases rather than diminishes the lovers' passion. Both write ardent letters which they never mail, love poetry which turns memories into desperation. After three months

Fernando can bear the separation no longer and returns to Madrid. He renews his affair with Dorotea, but jealousy drives him into a duel with his rival, Don Bela, and Fernando leaves him gravely wounded.

Reconciliation with Dorotea is once again destroyed when she learns about Fernando's intrigue with Marfisa. Don Bela, scarcely recuperated from his duel with Fernando, is attacked by bullies and killed. Dorotea, wearying of the alternating tortures and delights of worldly love, enters a convent seeking divine love. Fernando, depressed by the gloomy prognostications of an astrologer ("Great sorrows and troubles await you because of your love affairs . . ."), enlists in His Majesty's service with the Invincible Armada. Ironically Gerarda, the old procuress, now eighty years old, dies from a fall doing a small kindness for Dorotea—bringing her a glass of water.

In *La Dorotea* we have an eloquent example of what Carl Vossler calls the seventeenth-century Spaniard's practice of "turning life into literature and literature into life." Lope said in his dedication that he wrote it in his youth and redacted it in his old age; he published it only three years before his death. The work summarizes the most turbulent years of his amours with Elena Osorio, lays his soul (and hers) bare, and exasperates researchers, for the distinction between fiction and fact escapes the most learned *lopista*. In *La Dorotea* Lope compounds and mingles almost inexorably the story of his own amorous autobiography and that of the Spanish bawd, Celestina. For old Gerarda, hated and wheedled by the other characters, making her base living in the only way she knows how, as a procuress, is a very slightly modified copy of the Celestina from *The Tragicomedy of Calixto and Melibea*, 1499–1501, more often entitled *La Celestina*. Gerarda drinks to excess, spouts proverbs, quotes the Bible, can smell out a customer with a feline skill. Yet it would not be easy to ascertain how much of her Lope took from *La Celestina* and how much from actual experience with similar old crones, who probably flourished in the Madrid of his day. Instead of having her killed much like a beast, as occurs in the original *Celestina*, Lope gives her a peaceful departure from the world. After she passes safely through the homes of the well-to-do, through brothels, churches, and grog shops, she rushes all too rapidly for her eighty years to bring water to Dorotea who is in a faint, only to fall and die, as we said, doing a kindness. Celia, Dorotea's maid, pronounces a sort of funeral oration for the old woman somewhat in the mock spirit of the lower-class characters of the original *Celestina:*

God knows how wretched your death makes me feel; rest in peace, instructor in lovemaking, Seneca of eloquence, expert beggar, consultant in the art of giving, and the person who more than anyone else in the world understood the wiles of women and how to fleece men.

Fernando in *La Dorotea* mirrors an unmistakable reflection of Lope as a young man, of his blundering passionate certainties and uncertainties, his immaturity and inexperience, his ruthless search for sexual pleasure, his weaving of snares which tripped the weaver. He spent whole nights moonstruck at Dorotea's window in the winter—Madrid's infamous winter, which even the ancient proverb disparaged: "En Madrid, el viento no apaga un candil pero mata a un hombre" ("In Madrid the wind won't put out a candle but it will kill a man"). Yet under all these youthful faults of character lies the poet, the soldier, and the lonely man who could write these untranslatable lines:

A mis soledades voy,        (Back to loneliness I
de mis soledades vengo,      go although I just left
porque para andar conmigo   loneliness; my thoughts
me bastan mis pensamientos. . . .  are my sole company. . . .)

Although *La Dorotea* seems wordy to today's reader, its revelation of the nature of the sex life of Spain's Golden Age is a compensation for the painstaking reading required. In its way *La Dorotea* is a report on the sex life of male and female of both the hidalgo and the mass man of Lope's time. Its basic hypothesis, Freudian three hundred years before Freud, is found in these words from Act I, scene 5: "The tap root of all human emotions is sex: out of it come sadness, joy, ecstasy, exhilaration, and desperation."

Interest in Lope de Vega's *La Dorotea* (1632) has quickened in intensity in our day. Edwin S. Morby, editor of the University of California edition of *La Dorotea* (1958), considers it to be Lope's "richest, best-planned, most complex work, the one which best summarizes his capacities as a lyric poet, dramatist, and prose writer. . . ." Three modern editions have appeared since 1951. *La Dorotea* was, in Lope's own words, "la más querida" (the work he preferred above all others).

STORIES FOR MARCIA LEONARDA, *1621* AND *1624*. *Stories for Marcia Leonarda* (*Novelas a Marcia Leonarda*), four in number, were written at the urging of Lope's last love, Marta de Nevares (see Chapter 1, II), who was so impressed by the success of Cervantes with fiction that she hoped to inspire Lope to become a novelist. The stories are practically epistolary, with the author frequently addressing Marta directly and creating the effect of dialogue. Although they rank low in artistry on Lope's production scale, they interest us because they exhibit once again the influence of a woman on the work of the poet. He said he wrote *Stories for Mircia Leonarda* "in obedience to Marta." At the conclusion of the fourth story Lope promised a fifth, which never appeared. He once declared that he had no intention of becoming a novelist.

## II  *Narrative Poetry*

DRAKE THE PIRATE, *1598*. In the same year that *La Arcadia* appeared, Lope published in Valencia the epic poem *Drake the Pirate* (*La Dragontea*). Written in royal octaves (*octavas reales*), *La Dragontea* contains ten cantos which narrate the forays of Sir Francis Drake to the Canary Islands, Puerto Rico, Panama, Nombre de Dios, and Portobello. The poem concludes with the story of his death by poison administered by his own crew in Portobello.

*La Dragontea* is a colossal mediocrity. Góngora, Lope's great contemporary, said sarcastically, "What a small streak of lightning for such a loud clap of thunder . . . !" If Don Nadie (a nobody) had written it instead of a laureled poet, it would have disappeared without a trace. One can only plow through its wasteland of venom—heaped upon Queen Elizabeth I, Sir Francis Drake, Juan Achines (John Hawkins) and Protestantism—by means of herculean determination and a library of dictionaries of mythology, history, folklore, religion, nautical terminology, and theology.

Although it does not annotate or elucidate, the 1935 edition[5] indexes hundreds of names of boats, places, and persons historical, allegorical, and mythological. Lope intermingled world celebrities with many an unknown Juan del Pueblo (Joe Doaks). Entreating Venus to "leave him alone for a while," in Canto I, he took into his study the prosy documents on Drake from the *Real Audiencia* (Royal Tribunal) of Panama and turned them into eight-line stanzas. Before finishing he had allegorized the Christian Religion and "her three daughters, Spain, Italy and the New World," personified Madame Greed, raised a number of thorny theological questions, condemned to Hell all the heretics in Europe, boasted that the British lost seventeen thousand men in their raid on Cádiz, prayed to God to intervene personally to kill Drake, told of Drake's leaving a signed receipt (as a joke) for the 1,600,000 ducats of silver he stole from a Spanish galleon —and so on.

*La Dragontea* gloats over the death in 1596 of *el Draque* (Drake), so long a familiar though formidable figure throughout the Spanish-speaking world, but not even its timeliness could make it sell. The poem is a witches' brew of Spanish fury boiling up out of chauvinism and *odium theologicum*.

EL ISIDRO, *1599.* Lope published *El Isidro*[6] to glorify the life of Madrid's farmer patron saint. For this dum-de-dum poem, Lope used an old-fashioned, popular form of versification called the *quintilla* (a five-line stanza of octosyllabic lines using any rhyme scheme, except that no three consecutive lines must rhyme). A learned Spanish critic said *El Isidro* contained "a lot of mixed fodder and even rubbish," and I find it easy to subcribe to his opinion. Lope emphasized the humility of Isidro by repeating significantly, if monotonously, a vocabulary which seemed best to highlight folksiness in his rustic hero: "farmer, plow, sickle, ploughman, common man, rustic, poverty, poor table, poor swaddling clothes, poor bed, poor chairs, poor food." Dwelling upon Isidro's lack of book learning, Lope writes: "Isidro knew neither his letters nor anyone to teach them to him." Rhapsodically praised for living by the sweat of his brow, Isidro gets attention not only from the goddess Envy, and from the fallen-angel Satan, but from the Creator Himself.

With undisguised statistical pride, Lope proclaimed that whereas Abraham had only *three* angels appear to him, Isidro had *six*. Furthermore they plowed his fields for him. If metropolitan Madrid would go out in the country to find its patron saint, Lope approved wholeheartedly. By exalting him, Lope helped to lift the rustic Isidro to a place of pre-eminence in the religious world, and once more exalted the uncommon common man. *El Isidro* went through eight editions in the seventeenth century alone.[7]

ANGELICA'S BEAUTY, *1602. Angelica's Beauty* (*La hermosura de Angélica*),[8] published in Madrid (or Seville?), is a vexatiously long work, a hybrid poem without form, sense, or visible pattern. Lope claimed to have written most of it while he was with the expeditionary force of the Invincible Armada in 1588, and then to have laid it aside for some years before completing and publishing it. He said he hoped to compete with such epic poets as Ariosto and Luis Barahona de Soto. In so competing he produced a monstrous hodgepodge of mythology, personal amorous recollection, chauvinism, wailing against destiny's cruelty, and tiresome digression. Vossler, the Geman *lopista, says La hermosura de Angélica* makes no sense, and the public may have thought so too, for the book met a cool reception. It clangors with faults, as for example the absurd outflow—at times eruption—of names, now mostly unknown:

> Víanse luego Olimpia, Sacripante,
> Gravina, Marganor, Grifón, Bardino,
> Argalía, Guidón, Caligorante,
> León, Gradaso, Ferragut, Cervino,
> Malaligi, Bucífaro, Aquilante,
> Branzardo, Falerina, Urger, Sobrino,
> Atlante, Pinabelo, Sansoneto,
> Alcina, Logistila y Ricardeto.

In this poem, as repeatedly in others, Lope includes thinly veiled accounts of real love affairs. The plot, if the poem can be said to have one, narrates the trials of blonde Angélica and dark Medoro and their ill-starred destiny with a certain Nereida and Zerdano, pursued by the brutal Rostubaldo of Toledo. The protagonists are overshadowed repeatedly by secondary figures introduced kaleidoscopically into the poem.

The least dull incident in *Angelica's Beauty* is the story of the search for both Miss and Mr. Universe, in the International Beauty Contest. The prize offered is no less than "the throne of Seville." Contestants gather from the four corners of the earth. Lope describes the beauty of the women with sensual gusto, ridicules the effeminate male contestant who won first place—but without saying exactly why that contestant shouldn't have lost. In 1614 Lope collaborated with a composer to adapt *Angelica's Beauty* for stage performance with music, altering its title to *Reward for Beauty* (*El premio de la hermosura*).

JERUSALEM REGAINED, *1609.* In 1609 Lope published a prolix epic poem of six thousand stanzas entitled *Jerusalem Regained* (*Jerusalén conquistada*) and dedicated it to Felipe III. The poem purports to tell the history of the Third Crusade (1187–92). Lope arbitrarily includes Alfonso VIII of Castile (who never went) along with Richard the Lion Hearted of England and Philippe-Auguste of France. The content of *Jerusalem Regained* is summarized by Frank Pierce, author of *The Heroic Poem of the Spanish Golden Age: Selections,* New York—Toronto, 1947, p. 66:

The reader is conducted from Spain, where he witnesses the visit of Richard and his sister, who was to become the wife of Alfonso, through the Mediterranean to Cyprus and on to Palestine, where many engagements and encounters take place, culminating in rivalry and discord amongst the three monarchs, and the inglorious withdrawal of each in his turn, with Jerusalem still in the hands of the Saracens. . . . Into this broad canvass is woven a multiplicity of happenings and adventures, including the many love affairs and quarrels of the various warriors of the three main armies, pastoral episodes, scenes of enchantment, . . . allegorical passages, lineages, reviews of troops, prophecies and recapitulations. The main characters, apart from the trinity of leaders, are modelled to varying degrees on [characters] from Tasso's *Gerusalemme Liberata* . . . the Spanish captains, Garcerán Manrique and Garci Pacheco, who bluster their arrogant way through the poem, probably have more originality in their portrayal. Lope . . . reduces in number his heroes and heroines as against the galaxy of figures in the Italian model.[9]

Lope set great store by the success of *Jerusalem Regained,* his most ambitious single literary venture. He hoped to give Spain a great national epic poem to rival Portugal's *Os Lusiadas* (1572) of Camões. He had begun it in his youth and had returned through the years to its redaction and polishing. The dedication to the King, Lope's prolix notes, his pompous prologue, all speak for themselves in proclaiming the poet's considerable pride in his labors. He resented the Italian Tasso's having left Spaniards out of *Gerusalemme Liberata* and rectified this slight by supplying Spaniards for *Jerusalem Regained* out of his fancy. One of the most interesting fragments of the poem is Lope's description of the visit of the prideful Captain Pacheco to Saladin's headquarters. Pacheco takes arrogant liberties, including sitting down without Saladin's leave, boasting that a "Spaniard sits where and when he pleases." The poem contains a number of other similar blustering rodomontades.

*Jerusalem Regained* was reprinted in 1609, 1611, and 1619 and then not again until the eighteenth century. Before bringing it to the light of day, Lope suffered many vicissitudes, including harsh criticism from his contemporaries. The poem shows strong resemblance to the books of chivalry, featuring, as it does, angels, demons, magicians, and necromancers.

Joaquín de Entrambasaguas, in his edition[10] of the work published in 1951–54, says most critics have judged the poem too hastily. Entrambasaguas labored long to produce a faithful edition, containing both Lope's and his own profusion of notes, in order to make available a work he feels deserves fame rather than oblivion.

In Cantos VIII, XVI, and XVII Lope, again as was his custom, turned autobiography into poetry by portraying his current mistress, Micaela de Luján (Lucinda), and all five of their illegitimate children: Angela, Jacinta, Mariana, Juan, and Félix.

THE TRAGIC CROWN, *1627.* In *The Tragic Crown* (*La corona trágica*), Lope reflected Spain's affection, and his own, for Catholic Mary Stuart, Queen of Scots. It is the story of her tragic life. Lope states in the prologue that the source of his poem was a biography of Mary in Latin by a Dominican monk, Georgius Conaeus (George Conn), *Vita Mariae Stuartae Scotiae reginae, Angliae, et Hiberniae heredis,* (*The Life of Mary Stuart, Queen of Scotland and England, Heir to Ireland*) Rome, 1624. Lope's poem is a five thousand-line glorification of Mary and denunciation of Queen Elizabeth I. Motivated by two primal emotions, patriotism and *odium theologicum* (theologian's wrath), Lope calls Elizabeth by names of repulsive animals (hyena, tiger, snake), and of infamous women from the Bible and ancient mythology (Jezebel, Atropos, and Queen Semiramis of Babylon). Protestant critics generally call the poem dull, intolerant, distorted; Catholic critics are usually more generous.

It is not easy to judge the poem impartially. It was certainly well received in high Catholic circles in its time. Pope Urban VIII, to whom it was dedicated, sent Lope a personal letter of commendation and awarded him the title of Doctor of Theology plus the Cross of the Order of Saint John. Henceforth he signed himself *Fra* Lope de Vega.

THE WAR OF THE CATS, *1634.* The burlesque poem entitled *The War of the Cats* (*La gatomaquia*),[11] appeared first in a volume of miscellaneous poetry. It is a clever, although lengthy, parody of Italian epic poetry in seventy-eight hundred lines. The protagonists are personified cats. Lope patterned them after epic heroes and heroines. He made them speak a pompous language and display human characteristics. They are by turns learned, quarrelsome, boastful, passionate, and jealous. He scattered here and there the usual black magic, fanciful astrology, fierce combat, and love affairs.

The plot of *The War of the Cats* is spun around the turbulent love story of the heroine Zapaquilda and the hero Micifuf. Treacherous Marramaquiz, Micifuf's jealous rival, assisted by the magician Garfiñanto, attempts to seduce Zapaquilda by arousing her jealousy. He fails. Micifuf's ardor wins Zapaquilda, and their wedding day is set. Alas! At the wedding feast Marramaquiz kidnaps the bride and carries her off to his castle. Unhappy, but game and gritty, Micifuf storms the castle and finally captures it with the aid of the gods of Olympus. *Cattus ex machina.*

This feline parody has proved its lasting popularity in approximately twenty editions. One phase of its tongue-in-cheek wit is exemplified by its marvelously festive onomastics, such as *Mizifuf* (Snort), *Zapirón* (Scat), *Lameplatos* (Platelicker), and Lope's rollicking inventiveness of comic words, untranslatable, their chief value resting in their sound: *ñiñafe, ñiñiñaque, chipqui-chaque, zipizape.*

The Spanish essayist Azorín assessed *The War of the Cats* as the product of Lope's hitting back, in his old age, at jealousy, the emotion that had stung him so mercilessly during the whole of his long life. But for the editor of the 1935 edition of the poem, Francisco Rodríguez Marín, Lope was hiding, under a festive cat masquerade, a satire of the society of his day with its universal coquetry, senseless duels, fiestas, vanity, boundless pride of ancestry, deadbeat nobility, frivolous promises, and general moral breakdown. The cats were thinly disguised people.[12]

THREE LATE POEMS. Late in his career Lope de Vega wrote a number of narrative poems in which he was inclined to lecture to his reader. Three such poems are *The New Art of Play Writing in Our Time* (*El arte nuevo de hacer comedias en este tiempo,* Madrid, 1609), already commented upon in Chapter 3; *Introduction to the Royal Studies of the Society of Jesus* (*Isagoge a los Reales Estudios de la Compañía de Jesús,* Madrid, 1629); and *The Laurel of Apollo* (*El Laurel de Apolo,* Madrid, 1630).

In the *Isagoge,* an incidental work commemorating the dedication of a new building of the Imperial School of the Society of Jesus in Madrid, Lope invoked the muses, the regions and rivers of Spain, glorified teachers, and lavished hyperbole upon the King's powerful favorite, the Conde-Duque of Olivares.

The *Laurel of Apollo* is a free-handed enumeration and a full-hearted evaluation of 280 Spanish and Portuguese and 36 French and Italian poets, plus 24 "men of genius" of antiquity; and to complete the roundup, nine Spanish painters. The work surprises today's readers by the mediocrities Lope included, yet surprises them even more by the celebrities he omitted. He exhibits some traces of petulance; for example, Juan de la Cueva (1543–1610), a playwright of Lope's school, had published an *ars poetica* in 1606 and abstained from mentioning Lope; so in the *Laurel of Apollo* Lope abstained from mentioning Cueva.

Although the *Laurel of Apollo* consists of nearly seven thousand lines of indiscriminate praise, it is far from being merely a rhymed catalog, for it affords, in some ways, a mountaintop vista of Lope's tastes and preferences in literature and painting. Still, he was sensitive to the political values of his appraisals and may have praised persons who were to him "right" in their attitude, whether or not they were mediocre poets.

The *Laurel of Apollo* is built around a festival celebrated on Mt. Helicon by Apollo, who invited several hundred guests from Spanish-speaking countries everywhere, including the New World. Apollo held the kind of contest that only a god could manage: there were no losers! At the conclusion of the affair he awarded the laurel to Iris, who in turn bore it to King Felipe IV.

Lope offered the compensatory apology in the prologue to the *Apollo* that if he forgot anyone deserving of notice, it was purely unintentional. But it is difficult to comprehend the absence of Saint Teresa, and Saint John of the Cross, among others.

The *Apollo* is a characteristically Lopean miscellany in which the poet discloses his own ideas about writing by commenting upon metrics, poetic innovations from Italy, and the origin of certain Spanish verse forms from Latin. He also inserts into this miscellany bits of autobiography—an obvious reference to Marta de Nevares, another to their daughter, Antonia Clara—as well as a number of digressions, such as the fable of Narcissus, and that of Diana at the bath. More than once he expresses pride and satisfaction that poetry flourishes so remarkably in his native land.

We must consider Lope's numerous letters as a segment—and a considerable one—of his non-dramatic works, in particular his correspondence with the Duke of Sessa; belonging also to this category are his numerous officially written censures and approbations of literary works of his contemporaries, and many panegyrics and poems in anthologies. The number and quality of lost works are still unknown. Although Lope's non-dramatic works form only a fraction of his total production, those known to be his filled a twenty-one volume set published in the eighteenth century in Madrid (1776–79) and entitled *Colección de obras sueltas, así en prosa como en verso* (*Collection of Individual Works in Prose and Poetry*).

# CHAPTER 5

# *Representative Quotations and Maxims from Lope de Vega's Works Classified by Keyword*

LOPE de Vega's works teem with maxims, adages, and folk proverbs.[1] All fit appropriately into the pertinent content at hand, and at the same time achieve wide relevance through their universality. Like his contemporaries in Spanish drama, he often clothes these two-, three-, and four-line sententious phrases in striking metaphor. The metaphors reflect the life of a Spain leaderless and in decline. They reflect Lope's life, too, nourished upon the classics, the Middle Ages, and the truisms of his own generation.

The quotations below (the translations are mine) super-abound in references to *woman, honor, love, hate,* and *jealousy.* As might be expected, although quotations were selected at random, references to such volatile subject matter from the pen of an individual as volatile as Lope are far from tame. Many of them seem to flow straight from the poet's own erotic indiscretions and dalliances.

Most of the quotations cited are identified by scene as well as by act if from a play edited with those divisions; however, in the remainder, identification is given by play and act only where the play lacks division into scenes.

No secret ever revealed hurts more than that of one's AGE.
—*La Dorotea*, I, 1

Malice and envy—how characteristic of old AGE.
—*La Dorotea*, IV, 6

A philosopher once said that half of all BEAUTY is owing to the dress-maker.
—*The Dog in the Manger*, I, 12

Is not BEAUTY from age 15 to 25 a joyful spring, from 25 to 35 a pleasant summer, from 35 to 45 a doughty summer?
—*La Dorotea*, I, 1

What greater wealth can a woman have than to see herself immortalized in verse? BEAUTY fades, and when she is looked upon when faded, no one believes she ever had it; but poetry written in praise of her beauty is an eternal witness.

—*La Dorotea*, II, 2

✗ No woman's BEAUTY compares to a purse full of money.

—*Discreet Vengeance*

If You Can Do No BETTER [sleep with your own wife].

—Proverb and play title

If you're a BUTTER HEAD, don't become a baker.  —*La Dorotea*, III, 3

The Duke: The opinions of the COMMON MAN are unreliable and inconstant, unruled by reason.  —*Justice Without Revenge*, 1

It's advantageous for CATTLE to have the wolf's friendship.

—*The Reluctant Bride and Groom from Hornachuelos*, I

Felipa: [In love] where CONSENT goes not, the flesh walks alone, like one who carries a lantern lighting up the street but obscuring the lantern-bearer.  —*La Dorotea*, III, 8

Women and simpletons use COSMETICS to their own harm.

—*La Dorotea*, V, 10

COURAGE is the equivalent of many soldiers.

—*Man Who Looked for Trouble*, I, 5

Spend your time with the CRAZY set and you will end up crazy yourself.  —*The Adventures of Man* (one-act Eucharistic play)

Something other than the passing of the years brings a man gray hair and CUCKOLDRY.  —*The Great Captain's Bookkeeping*, III

Teodoro: How shall I CURE my lovesickness?

Tristán: By dwelling upon her defects, forgetting her charms.

—*The Dog in the Manger*, I, 22

Agile, nimble DEATH, who levels us each and everyone.

—*Comedia of Bamba*, II

Distance is the best truce in any DISPUTE.  —*Peribáñez*, III

The DONKEY [i.e., foolish person] who showers praise upon other donkeys deserves to have a donkey for a son.  —*La Dorotea*, I, 1

Our DREAMS arise from what we've done or what we wish to do; and so the virtuous dream better dreams than the evil, the vicious, and the perverse.  —*La Dorotea*, I, 4

EAT what and as you please but let your speech and clothes strictly follow fashion.  —*La Dorotea*, I, 7

Only a fool awakens his sleeping ENEMY. —*Awakening the Sleeper*, I, 6

Fame is the light, ENVY merely its shadow.

—*The Great Captain's Bookkeeping*, I

There is no EVIL so heinous that human frailty cannot compass it.

—*Justice Without Revenge*, III

FATE is a blind woman so unsteady on her feet that her clogs are like
wheels. —*Poverty Is No Disgrace*, III

Aurora: The sweetest FAVORS are never granted at the first approach,
but reserved until love is tested and trusted.
—*Love Without Revenge*, II

Celia: More women have been led astray through the ears than
through the eyes; they've always been harmed more by listening
to FLATTERY than by the sight of elegance and beauty.
—*La Dorotea*, V, 9

FLATTERY makes prairies of mountains. —*The Star of Seville*, III, 13

Blind FORTUNE tomorrow humiliates whom she exalted today.
—*The Sheepwell*, II

FRIENDLINESS softens a woman's hard scorn.
—*Poverty Is No Disgrace*, III

Even if a blow with a FRYING PAN doesn't hurt, it leaves a dirty stain.
—*La Dorotea*, III, 3

FRIENDS generally fail you in a tight spot.
—*The Girl With the Pitcher*, I, 14

FRIENDSHIP is not possible without social equality.
—*The Girl With the Pitcher*, II, 8

The most singular charm of both men and women is their GAIT.
—*La Dorotea*, II, 1

It's magnanimous in a man to be GALLANT toward all women . . . for
they all deserve love, and a 'one and only' is nonsense.
—*Perseverance Triumphs Over Love*, I, 5

GIFTS open the door to women's favors. —*The Star of Seville*, I

It's better to believe in GOD than try to understand Him.
—*Unstained Purity* (one-act Eucharistic play)

There's no weapon of defense against GOLD. —*La Dorotea*, IV, 1

GOLD is like women: everybody vilifies them but everybody desires
them. —*La Dorotea*, I, 4

No one in sound health GOSSIPS. —*The Girl With the Pitcher*, III, 7

No force can match divine GRACE and free will. —*La Dorotea*, I, 6

What is GRIEF for one is joy for another.
—*The Reluctant Bride and Groom From Hornachuelos*, II

There is as much HAPPINESS in a poor man's as in a royal bed—for all
love is equal in the dark, whatever its lineage.
—*Justice Without Revenge*, II

HARMONY is composed of opposites. —*La Dorotea*, V, 3

The HEART has doors through which it is entered and stolen.
—*La Dorotea*, II, 5

HONOR, cruel enemy of mankind! —*Justice Without Revenge*, III

Oh, HONOR, thou art made of glass, and the weakest blow breaks the
strongest glass. *—Peribáñez,* II

HONOR is always to be preferred over love. *—Madrid Bouquets,* II, 6

The King of Ireland: Francelisa, run along back to your maids and
your knitting . . . you women don't understand the business of
HONOR. *—Don Juan de Castro,* 2nd part, II, 4

Duke: A man whose HONOR has been publicly avenged carries with
him some trace of the foulness which stained it . . . So no living
soul must know of my vengeance. *—Justice Without Revenge,* III

Queen (to her subject, García): Live! I condemn you to life although
I could send you to your death; but there's no greater punish-
ment than extending life to a man who has lost his HONOR.
*—Testimony Avenged,* III

The King of Ireland: HONOR is from God alone: whatever is an offense
to God is dishonorable. *—The Poignant Force,* II

Until the wedding night, the HONOR of a woman is the father's obligation, not the husband's. *—The Sheepwell,* III

Blanca: Husbands lie sleepless more nights because of HONOR than of
love. *—Honor Struggle,* I

Never make anything—not even an inkwell—of HORNS. [Horns were
the sign of cuckoldry.] *—Peribáñez,* I

There is no HOUSE without its skeleton closet. *—La Dorotea,* III, 3

Dorotea: I'm ILL from a troubled spirit—not from any distemper of
the blood. *—La Dorotea,* II, 2 [An anticipation of the theory of
psychosomatic illness.]

Casandra: I wonder why Heaven gave man the power of IMAGINA-
TION. It confounds reason, turns our firmest resolve into ashes.
Imagination turns fire into frost, transforms all things to the
shapes desire would have them take. Imagination is a kind of
spirit that deceives more than it enlightens.
*—Justice Without Revenge,* II

One in love should praise his beloved's IMPERFECTIONS . . . her
charms will praise themselves. *—Faithful Unto Death,* I

INDIGNATION makes the impossible possible. *—La Dorotea,* II, 3

Aurora: Where love is not, JEALOUSY makes no mark.
*—Justice Without Revenge,* III

Nuño: It's silly to trust the illusions born of JEALOUSY because it transforms white into black. *—The Man Who Looked for Trouble,* II, 12

Nuño: Love, they say you won't budge unless shod with spurs by
JEALOUSY. *—The Man Who Looked for Trouble,* I, 9

The most discreet woman, when JEALOUS, loses her bearings.
*—The Man Who Looked for Trouble,* III, 3

Angela: JEALOUSY and love have an indivisible companionship, and I suspect they essentially are one, yet with this single difference—that jealousy is dark night, love daylight.
*—The Man Who Looked for Trouble,* II, 9

Fernando: Oh, JEALOUSY, tyrannical monarch, love's bastard!
*—La Dorotea,* III, 9

A JUDGE passes sentence with a heavy heart if he is guilty of the same crime. *—La Dorotea,* I, 1

Gerarda: The same KNIFE cuts my bread that cuts my finger.
*—La Dorotea,* II, 6

Gerarda: Trout and LIES, the bigger the better. *—La Dorotea,* IV, 6

LIFE is a dream. *—The Perils of Man* (One-act Eucharistic play)

Dorotea: What does LIFE turn out to be but a road to death?
*—La Dorotea,* V, 10

Casilda: I fear the LIGHTNING, not the thunder. *—Peribáñez,* III

LOVE is a desire for beauty. *—The Sheepwell,* I; *La Dorotea,* V, 3

LOVE is boldness, daring, abandon. *—Toledan Night,* II, 1

LOVE enters through the eyes. *—Toledan Night,* II, 3

The source of all the passions is LOVE: from it spring sadness, joy, happiness, and desperation. *—La Dorotea,* I, 5

Rodrigo: All things that live are born of LOVE and live by love; all things that die do so at the hand of a relentless power that undoes our lives. *—The Knight From Olmedo,* I

Without LOVE the world could not go on. *—The Sheepwell,* I

LOVE and war admit license. *—Awakening the Sleeper,* I, 18

No disturbance of the mind is more vehement than the fury of LOVE.
*—La Dorotea,* IV, 3

The grain of LOVE will bear no fruit unless it is sown with money.
*—Peribáñez,* I, 12

Nothing increases LOVE like an impassible hindrance.
*—Faithful Unto Death,* I, 21

All delight is sorrow, all pleasure torment; for even the truest LOVE turns to hate. *—La Dorotea,* V, final poem.

LOVE is not cured with herbs. *—La Arcadia,* Book V.

Batín [comedian]: Thoughts on LOVE are like buckets on a waterwheel—as one bucket empties the water out, the next bucket scoops it up. *—Justice Without Revenge,* II

Fernando: LOVE is not a shadow which vanishes with the body.
*—La Dorotea,* I, 5

Juan: I also LOVE your soul, for love is not all carnal.
*—The Lady With the Pitcher,* II, 7

LOVE without a touch of madness is certain to fail.
*—The Man Who Looked for Trouble,* I, 10

Fernando: The pleasures of LOVE are wanton, fleeting, hollow dreams, forever diminished when achieved, magnified only when imagined. —*La Dorotea*, III, I

No one has any LOVE save for his own person. —*The Sheepwell*, I

There is no such thing as LOVE. —*The Sheepwell*, I

LOVE disperses darkness, makes the dumb speak, and turns fools into philosophers. —*Miss Simpleton*, III

A man in LOVE leaps easily over hills and oceans. —*The Sheepwell*, II

Nuño: Returning scorned LOVE with scorn satisfies almost as much as receiving love. —*The Man Who Looked for Trouble*, II, 11

LOVE is idleness, leisure; no busy man ever found love, no idle man ever failed to find it. —*La Arcadia*, Book V

LOVE finds entrance easy, exit hard. —*La Dorotea*, I, 5

LOVE?—Paint it in the multicolored costume of a madman, and call it *habit*. —*La Dorotea*, I, 5

The first step towards LOVE is respect.
—*The Girl With the Pitcher*, II, 1

Dorotea: LOVE is no pearl intended for dunces, but seeks subtle minds, loathes selfishness, walks naked; it is not for the mean and shallow.
—*La Dorotea*, II, 2

LOVE, an absolute monarch, acknowledges only one law: *anything goes.*
—*The Girl With the Pitcher*, III, 12

LOVE is repaid only in kind. —*Miss Simpleton*, I, 13

Let no man say he is in LOVE if he feels no jealousy.
—*La Arcadia*, Book I

Fernando: LOVE is deeds, not words. —*La Dorotea*, IV, 1

Dorotea: LOVE and honor dislike advice. —*La Dorotea*, IV, 1

Gerarda: LOVE and authority dislike company. —*La Dorotea*, IV, 66

Dorotea: LOVE and fear were born of the same delivery.
—*La Dorotea*, IV, 1

I believe a cultured man LOVES deepest, because the man who knows most feels most. —*The Mayor*, II

A fool is incapable of LOVE. —*The Merlons of Toro*, II

Dorotea: Anger and LOVE are our two dominant emotions [i.e., in women]. —*La Dorotea*, V, 9

LOVE must be free; it may not be forced.
—*Justice Without Revenge*, III

LOVE is not governed by reason. —*The Discreet Man Chastises*

In LOVE lying and telling the truth are the same.
—(Letter to the Duke of Sessa)

All things are within the grasp of the lover who seeks them with LOVE.
—*Punishment Without Vengeance*, II

Fernando: The falling out of lovers means the restoration of LOVE.
                                           —*La Dorotea*, V, 3

All [five] senses of a man in LOVE are in his imagination.
                                           —*La Dorotea*, III, 5

Ludovico: The sickness of LOVE is cured with baths, music, wine, and
   going to the theater.              —*La Dorotea*, III, 4

Florencio: For woman-sickness (i.e. LOVEsickness), a man purges himself—with another woman: the antidote.

Lisena: Woman cure womanitis? Well!

Florencio: Sure . . . fight poison with poison.
                                           —*Toledan Night*, I, 18

LOVE, eating, and scratching prick only at the start.
                                           —*Toledan Night*, I, 6

A LOVER loves even his beloved's dog.        —*Lucky Revenge*, II

Our Spanish language admits only one small letter between MARRIED
   (*casado*) and TIRED (*cansado*).        —*La Dorotea*, I, 6

Aurora: MARRIAGE must be made by free choice.
                                           —*Justice Without Revenge*, III

Many MARRY in haste and repent at leisure.
                                           —*The Girl With the Pitcher*, I, 1

There is no rein like MARRIAGE to keep a man in check . . .
                                           —*Justice Without Revenge*, I

The world's fiercest storms are those within the MIND.
                                           —*Justice Without Revenge*, II

A virtuous maiden's duty to be MODEST increases in proportion to her
   beauty.              —*The War of the Cats*, first *silva*.

MONEY is the traveler's feet.        —*Awakening the Sleeper*, III, 4

When Señor MONEY walks out on you, most of your friends go with
   him.              —*The Great Captain's Bookkeeping*, II

Señor MONEY Is a Very Fine Gentleman.        —Title of a play

Make no mistake about it, MONEY is all in all: it is prince, noble, gentleman, blue-blood, descended from the Goths [i.e., of ancient and
   proud ancestry.]              —*The Test of Friendship*

Fernando (to Dorotea): Our [men's] first MOTHERLAND is women,
   and we never leave you.              —*La Dorotea*, I, 5

All that NATURE gives us is on loan.        —*La Dorotea*, III, 3

Lawless NECESSITY is in the driver's seat [of life].
                                           —*Poverty Is No Disgrace*, I

All this NOBILITY stuff is pure fabrication.        —*Village Nobility*, I

Gerarda: We PARENTS are like birds: once our little birds learn to fly,
   we let the air—and them with their own beaks—support them.
                                           —*La Dorotea*, I, 1

Adorning a wall with PICTURES is adorning it with ghosts.
*—Peribáñez,* II, 23

The PITCHER that goes often to the well is finally broken.
*—The Girl With the Pitcher,* II, 14

There is no PLEASURE which does not have pain at its periphery.
*—La Dorotea,* III, 2

Dorotea: POETS are men
    steeped in sin;
    their wares: impossibilities.    *—La Dorotea,* II, 5

Where a POOR man would be called a fool, a rich man is called a
    philosopher.       *—Miss Simpleton,* I, 12

Pity a POOR man if he marries a beautiful wife.   *—Peribáñez,* II, 16

For whom does the blind man's wife PRIMP?    *—La Dorotea,* IV, 6

The REMEMBRANCE of princes . . . lies in the writers' pen.
*—La Dorotea,* III, 5

A closed book produces no SCHOLARS.     *—La Dorotea,* I, 1

The distance between the SOUL and the tongue is greater than between
    heaven and earth.      *—Justice Without Revenge,* II

TEARS not born of love are usually counterfeit.
*—The Man Who Looked for Trouble,* II, 20

Fernando: Women's TEARS are mere heartstrings to their laughter. Not
    even a summer shower dries up faster.    *—La Dorotea,* I, 5

In what mirror can a lover see himself better reflected than in TEARS,
    for are they not the living mirror of the soul?  *—La Dorotea,* I, 5

Casandra: TEARS are women's realm, who, though their hearts be
    courageous, lack the strength to right their wrongs. Men ought
    to show firm resolve to weep for one cause alone—the loss of
    honor.       *—Justice Without Revenge,* II

TIME generally cures the incurable.   *—The Girl With the Pitcher,* I, 4

Naked TRUTH is clothed stupidity.
*—The Reluctant Bride and Groom From Hornachuelos,* I

TRUTH fosters a bitter spirit.   *—The Great Captain's Bookkeeping,* III

UNDERSTANDING is the chief treasure of the soul.   *—Peribáñez,* II, 4

VIRTUE contains everything within itself and if you lack that you lack
    everything.        *—La Arcadia,* Book 5

Duke: The common man is always the greatest sufferer from WAR.
*—Justice Without Revenge,* I

Pierres (a belligerent monk): The elements are at WAR, as are all liv-
    ing things . . . Scarce were the angels created when there was
    war in Heaven, and even in sleep man is at war.
*—Life of St. Peter Nolasco,* I

The more WINE flows in, the more secrets flow out.
*—La Dorotea,* II, 6

Casandra: Take my advice—however chaste and guarded be a
WOMAN's fortress, you'll find its doors are made of wax.
*—Justice Without Revenge,* II

Marcela: Any intelligent man knows that the fragile glass of a
WOMAN's faith ought never be put to the test.
*—The Dog in the Manger,* II

How wise the man who flatters WOMEN, how stupid the one who trusts
them. *—Justice Without Revenge,* III

WOMEN are more likely to go wrong because ill-advised by their women
friends than because of their own weaknesses.
*—La Dorotea,* V, 3

Some WOMEN surrender easily to gain carnal satisfaction, for the philosopher [Aristotle] tells us they long for men as form yearns for
matter. *—The Sheepwell,* II

It's WOMAN's nature to spurn the man who pursues her.
*—The Sweetheart Spurned,* III

A WOMAN can tame the wildest and most arrogant man.
*—Justice Without Revenge,* I

Laurencio: A WOMAN and an orchard admit only one possessor.
*—La Dorotea,* III, 3

Julio: Ignorant WOMEN love the body, intelligent women the mind.
*—La Dorotea,* III, 7

Angela: The most intelligent and most stable of WOMEN, once she errs,
the error pursues her for life.
*—The Man Who Looked for Trouble,* III, 10

One cannot be sure of a WOMAN by guarding her.
*—The Discreet Man Chastises,* III

WOMAN and inconstancy are identical words.
*—The War of the Cats,* Book III, verse 229

✠Federico: The sweetest revenge upon a WOMAN is to let her have her
way. *—Justice Without Revenge,* II

Batín [comedian]: It was a wonderful device of nature to make
WOMEN deceitful. Had she made them faithful, men who adore
them now would worship them as idols of perfection.
*—Justice Without Revenge,* II

The luck of the plain WOMAN [is to have charm]. *—Peribáñez,* I

God preserve the tinder, WOMAN, from the raging fire, man.
*—Miss Simpleton,* III

Where anywhere will you find more war than in guarding a WOMAN?
*—Poverty Is No Disgrace,* I

An old WOMAN dancing raises a lot of dust. *—La Dorotea,* I, 7

There are no rules in a WOMAN's love nor certainty in the wind.
*—La Arcadia,* Book 1

*[ 129 ]*

# Notes and References

### Preface

1. Jacinto Benavente. *Obras completas (Complete Works)*. Madrid: Aguilar, 1958, Vol. XI, p. 608. All translations are the present author's unless otherwise indicated.

With regard to the indifference of the Spanish, and the zeal of the British, for publicizing the abode of their greatest dramatists respectively, the contrast between a trip to Stratford-on-Avon and a visit to the house of Lope de Vega on Cervantes Street in Madrid brings home to the foreign visitor the bizarre distance separating British from Spanish publicity practices. In England a visit to Shakespeare's home is thrust upon one from all sides with such genuine ardor—albeit somewhat business-like—that one feels guilt-ridden if he fails to go there, whereas in Madrid, in a recent visit to Lope's house (*la casa de Lope de Vega*), my two companions and I felt as if we were running a mile-long obstacle course just to obtain tickets, and then had trouble finding the house. Once there, after a knock on the street door, the custodian peered out at us to ask our business. When identified and granted entrance, we were treated with the courtesy Spaniards are famous for. But we were the only sightseers in Lope's house during the lengthy duration of our visit.

2. Federico Carlos Sáinz de Robles. *Lope de Vega—Retrato, horóscopo, vida y transfiguración*. Madrid: Espasa-Calpe, 1962, p. 7.
3. Azorín. *Lope en silueta*. Buenos Aires: Editorial Losada, S. A., 1960, pages 12–13.
4. Azorín, *loc. cit.*
5. Translated into Spanish, with additions and corrections, as *Vida de Lope de Vega*, Madrid, 1919, by Américo Castro.

### Chronology

1. S. Griswold Morley and Courtney Bruerton. *The Chronology of Lope de Vega's Plays*. Modern Language Association of America, Mon-

ograph Series no. XI, New York, 1940, p. 427. For additional information by the same authors, see *Hispanic Review*, XV (1947), Schevill Memorial Number.

2. W. T. McCready. "Lope de Vega's Birth Date and Horoscope." *Hispanic Review*, XXVIII, 313–18. The date given by Lope's friend, Juan Pérez de Montalbán, was November 25. There is no documentary evidence to support this. McCready gives irrefutable evidence that Montalbán erred and that Lope was born December 2 (old style), or December 12 (new style, Gregorian Calendar), 1562.

3. The authorship of *La Estrella de Sevilla* is in doubt, as is also the date of its composition; see S. E. Leavitt, *The Estrella de Sevilla and Claramonte*, Cambridge, Mass., 1931; Frank Otis Reed and Esther M. Dixon, editors, *La Estrella de Sevilla* with Introduction by John M. Hill. New York: D. C. Heath and Co., 1939.

### Chapter One

1. F. C. Sáinz de Robles, *op. cit.*, Chapter V.

2. *Ibid.*, Chapter V.

3. Joaquín de Entrambasaguas y Peña, *Vida de Lope de Vega*. Madrid: Editorial Labor, 1942, reimpresión, p. 48 *et seq.* In 1946, in a subsequent study entitled *Vivir y crear de Lope de Vega*, Madrid, Volume I, Entrambasaguas stated in his prologue that his *Vida de Lope de Vega* was reprinted without his supervision, contained errors and omissions, and was badly in need of correction and revision.

4. "Sobre un amor de Lope de Vega desconocido." *Revista de Filología Española*, XXV (1941), 103–08.

5. F. C. Sáinz de Robles, *op. cit.*, p. 84.

6. Joaquín de Entrambasaguas. *Vivir y Crear* . . . , I, pp. 188–89.

7. Thornton Wilder locates Micaela de Luján's husband in Spain some years after he was supposed to have left for Peru. See Courtney Bruerton, "Thornton Wilder and Lope's *Peregrino* Lists," *Bulletin of the Comediantes*, III, (1951) No. 1, 1.

8. F. C. Sáinz de Robles, *op. cit.*, p. 153.

9. J. de Entrambasaguas. *Vivir y Crear*, I, pp. 354–55.

10. Alonso Zamora Vicente. *Lope de Vega, su vida y su obra*. Madrid: Editorial Gredos, 1961, p. 84 *et. seq.*

11. LOPE AND WOMEN

| Name and Approximate Date of Relationship or Marriage | Lope's Nickname for Her | Children |
| --- | --- | --- |
| 1. Unknown woman (married)?, 1579 | Marfisa | |
| 2. Unknown woman (Lisbon), 1588 | | |
| 3. Elena Osorio 1583–87 (?) | Dorotea Filis | |
| 4. Isabel de Urbina Lope's *first wife* Married 1588; Died 1594 | Belisa | Antonia and Teodora (both died in infancy) |
| 5. Antonia Trillo de Armenta, 1596 (?) | | |
| 6. Micaela de Luján 1598?–1607? | Lucinda, Camila Lucinda | Agustina? Mariana? Angela, Lope Félix (Lopito), Jacinta, Marcela, Juan |
| 7. Flora (unidentified, 1602) | | |
| 8. Juana de Guardo, *second wife*. Married 1598; died 1613 | | Jacinta; Carlos Félix; a stillborn child; Feliciana |
| 9. Woman in Valencia (unidentified), 1599 | | Fernando Pellicer (Fray Vicente) |
| 10. Jerónima de Burgos 1613 | La señora Gerarda | |
| 11. Lucía de Salcedo, 1616 | "la loca" | |
| 12. Marta de Nevares, about 1617 until her death, 1632 | Amarilis Marcia Leonarda | Antonia Clara, 1617–44. Unmarried |
| 13. Unknown woman | | Fray Luis de la Madre de Dios |

## Chapter Two

1. J. E. Varey and N. D. Shergold. "Datos históricos sobre los primeros teatros de Madrid: contratos de arriendo, 1587–1615," *Bulletin*

*Hispañique,* LX, (1958), 73–95; LXII (1960), 163–89; 286–325. Concerning the popularity of the theater among numerous small-town audiences in the Madrid-Toledo area, see Noël Salomon, "Sur les représentations Théâtrales dans les 'pueblos' des Provinces de Madrid et Tolède (1589–1640)," *Bulletin Hispanique,* LXII (1960), 398–427.

2. Ruth Lundelius. *Physical Aspects of the Spanish Stage in the Time of Lope de Vega.* (Private edition, mimeographed) University of Pennsylvania, Philadelphia, 1961.

3. Wm. R. Weaver, "Introductory Study of Stage Devices in the *Siglo de oro* Drama," unpublished doctoral dissertation, University of North Carolina, Chapel Hill, 1936. I am also indebted to Wm. H. Shoemaker, *The Multiple Stage in Spain During the Fifteenth and Sixteenth Centuries,* Princeton: Princeton University Press, 1935; and Hugo A. Rennert, *The Spanish Stage in the Time of Lope de Vega,* New York: Dover Publications, 1963. (Reprint of the 1909 edition of the Hispanic Society of America, with some omissions).

4. Carmen Bravo-Villasante. *La mujer vestida de hombre en el teatro español, siglos XVI–XVII.* Madrid: Revista de Occidente, 1955.

5. For a summary of what is surely known, and what is speculated about Tirso's life and works, see Gerald E. Wade, "Tirso de Molina," *Hispania,* XXXII (May, 1949).

6. For four plays of his in English, see Edwin Honig, *Calderón, Four Plays,* Hill and Wang, New York, 1961. For those who read Spanish, easily available and recommended is Sturgis E. Leavitt's edition of *La vida es sueño* and *El alcalde de Zalamea,* Laurel Languages Library, Dell Publishing Co., New York, 1964.

7. Raymond R. MacCurdy. *Francisco de Rojas. Morir pensando matar. La vida en el ataúd.* Espasa-Calpe (*Clásicos Castellanos*), Madrid, 1961, Vol. 153, p. xvii.

8. Smith College, 1932.


*Chapter Three*

1. See, for example, E. Correa Calderón and Fernando Lázaro, *Lope de Vega y su época,* Madrid, 1961, Chapter 17.

2. See Francis C. Hayes. "The Use of Proverbs as Titles and Motives in The *Siglo de Oro* Drama: Lope de Vega." *Hispanic Review,* VI (1938), p. 305–23.

3. Ricardo del Arco y Garay. *La sociedad española en las obras dramáticas de Lope de Vega.* Madrid, 1941, p. 9 ff.

4. *Ibid.,* page 3.

5. For divergent views on how accurately Lope reflected the life

around him, see Américo Castro, *Tirso de Molina,* Clasicos Castellanos, Madrid, 1922, Vol. 2, pp. x–xliv; *Revista de Filología Española,* XV (1928), pp. 182–86; Rudolph Schevill, *The Dramatic Art of Lope de Vega,* University of California Press, Berkeley, 1918, p. 10 ff.

6. Robert Reid Morrison. "Sainthood in the Theater of Lope de Vega." Ph.D. dissertation, unpublished. University of Florida, Gainesville, 1963.

7. Adolfo Federico, Conde de Schack. *Historia de la literatura y del arte dramático en España,* traducida . . . del alemán . . . por Eduardo de Mier. Madrid: Colección Escritores Castellanos, 1885–87, Vol. 3, pp. 186–88.

8. Angel Valbuena Prat. *La religiosidad popular de Lope de Vega.* Madrid: Ateneo, 1963, 29 pages.

9. Other researchers support Cotarelo's stand; J. Entrambasaguas, for example, in *Lope de Vega y su tiempo,* Madrid, 1962, Vol. I, p. 308, points out that not a single contemporary of Lope, not even his enemies, contested the figure of eighteen hundred plays. Still, one of the knotty problems remaining is the authenticity of plays attributed to him: see J. H. Arjona, "The Plays Attributed to L. de V.," *Hispanic Review,* XXVIII (1960), 319–40; also studies by Walter Poesse, W. L. Fichter; S. G. Morley, "Lope de Vega's Prolificity and Speed," *Hispanic Review,* X (1942), pp. 67–68; Morley & Bruerton chronology, *op. cit.*

10. Lope wrote to his son, Lope Félix, in the dedication of *The True Lover* (*El verdadero Amante,* published in 1620): "I have written 900 plays, 12 books in prose and verse on diverse subjects, and so many unpublished pages on various subjects that what's already published will never equal what's still in manuscript; and I have gathered [on the way] censures, snares, envy, notes, scoldings, and worries, and wasted precious time."

11. Emilio Cotarelo y Mori, "Sobre el caudal dramático de Lope de Vega y sobre su desaparición y pérdida," *Boletín de la Academia Española,* XXII (1935), pp. 555–67.

12. S. Griswold Morley and Courtney Bruerton, "How many *comedias* did Lope de Vega write," *Hispania,* XI (1936), pp. 217–34; also S. Griswold Morley, "Lope de Vega's Prolificity and Speed," *Hispanic Review,* X (1942), pp. 67–8.

13. "The Chronology of Lope de Vega's *comedias,*" Modern Language Association of America, New York, 1940; for additional information by the same authors, see the *Hispanic Review,* XV (1947), Schevill Memorial Number.

14. See *The New Art of Writing Plays,* translated by Wm. T.

Brewster, in *Papers on Playmaking,* Edited by Brander Matthews. New York: Dramabooks, 1957.

15. J. Entrambasaguas y Peña, *Una guerra literaria del siglo de oro. Lope de Vega, y los preceptistas aristotélicos,* Madrid, 1932.

16. Ramón Menéndez Pidal, "Lope de Vega. *El arte nuevo* y la nueva biografía." *Revista de Filogogía Española,* XXII (1935), pp. 377–98.

17. M. Menéndez Pelayo, *Historia de las ideas estéticas en España,* Madrid, 1883–91, Vol. 2, pp. 294 *et seq.* (Enlarged to 9 vols. 1890–1907.)

18. Rinaldo Froldi, in *Il Teatro Velenzano E l'Origine Della Commedia Barocca,* Pisa, 1962, offers new evidence that the formula for the Golden Age play had its origin in Valencia. Froldi thinks that Andrés Rey de Artieda, Cristóbal de Virués, and particularly Francisco Agustín Tárrega, founded the Spanish comedia.

19. Alonso Zamora Vicente, *op. cit.,* p. 171.

20. Quoted by permission from *Lope de Vega (Five Plays),* translated by Jill Booty. Edited with an Introduction by R. D. F. Pring-Mill. New York: A Mermaid Dramabook, Hill and Wang, 1961: *The Knight of Olmedo,* Act II.

21. Diego Marín. *Uso y función de la versificación dramática en Lope de Vega.* Valencia: Editorial Castalia, 1962. The comments below on prevailing forms of verse employed by Lope are based on Marín's monograph.

*Romance* (ballad): most commonly used form; eight-syllable line and, beginning with the second line, every other line is in assonance. Assonance occurs in English in the saying "See a pin and pick it up, all day long you'll have good luck"; here *up* and *luck* are in assonance rather than rhyme. In the *romance,* or ballad, when the final word in the line is not accented on its last syllable, both the accented syllable and the last syllable must be in assonance. In his early years Lope used the *romance* for exposition and non-amorous subject matter, but from around 1600 on he almost constantly used it for expressing scenes of love and jealousy.

*Redondilla:* eight-syllable quatrain with rhyme *abba* or *abab;* especially used for dialogue, and sometimes "factual" rather than lyrical monologue; utilized for comic effect as well as for both happy and ill-starred love.

*Quintilla:* five-line stanza of eight syllables and two rhymes; there may not be three consecutive lines in rhyme; commonly used where feeling and emotion, rather than action, are to be highlighted, especially in the latter years of Lope's life.

*Décimas:* combines two *quintillas;* usually, there is a fixed rhyme arrangement of *abbaaccddc,* a pause in the sense after the fourth line. It was used little by Lope until late in life; he thought it good for emotional lyrical soliloquies and lovers' complaints.

*Octavas:* eight lines of eleven syllables with the rhyme scheme *abababcc;* most extensively used form from the Italian; most commonly employed for factual dialogue; associated with significant events; express noble sentiments without bombast; only sporadically used for lyrical soliloquies.

*Endecasílabos sueltos:* eleven-syllable free verse; early a favorite of the Italian meters used by Lope; later in his career frequently succeeded by *octavas;* expressed grave situations of dramatic intensity, or factual dialogue.

*Terceto:* eleven-syllable line; the first line is in consonance with the third line and the second line is in consonance with the first line of the following stanza; relatively less frequently used than other forms; recommended by Lope in *The New Art of Play Writing* to express grave situations, and so used, as well as for giving factual information.

*Silva:* an indefinite series of seven- and eleven-syllable lines which usually alternate; first line may rhyme with the second, the third with the fourth, or an alternate scheme at the will of the poet; has a variety of uses, such as factual dialogue, uneasiness, dramatic tension, and even for comic effect.

*Lira:* a not frequently occurring five-line stanza with seven syllables in the first, third, and fourth line and eleven syllables in the other two; sometimes there are six lines of varying length, the first four rhyming alternately, the last two rhyming with each other. It may express thoughts of lofty tone or, on the contrary, of rustic humor; this heightens the humor because the form is felt to be inappropriate for humor; also used to express love and jealousy.

*Canción:* a relatively rare verse form, generally of thirteen lines: *abcabccdeedff;* sometimes of eleven or nine lines in length; used principally for monologues, both for exposition and for expressing lofty sentiments.

A clear, brief explanation in English of Spanish verse forms, with examples, is to be found in Sturgis E. Leavitt's edition of two plays of Pedro Calderón de la Barca, *La Vida es sueño* and *El Alcalde de Zalamea,* Spanish Series, New York: The Laurel Language Library, 1964, pp. 16–18.

22. E. Correa Calderón and Fernando Lázaro. *Lope de Vega y su época.* Salamanca-Madrid: Ediciones Anaya, 1961, Vol. I, p. 107. (Vol. II contains an annotated edition of *El villano en su rincón.*)

23. S. Griswold Morley and Richard W. Tyler. *Los nombres de personajes en las comedias de Lope de Vega. Estudio de onomatología.* Valencia: Editorial Castalia, 1961. 2 vols.

24. A. A. Parker. "The Approach to the Spanish Drama of the Golden Age," *Tulane Drama Review,* IV (1959), pp. 42–59.

25. I am indebted for much of the material on honor to George T. Northup, ed., *Three Plays by Calderón,* New York: D. C. Heath, 1926, pp. xvi–xxiv.

26. Rudolph Schevill. *The Dramatic Art of Lope de Vega.* Berkeley: University of California Press, 1918, with an edition of *La dama boba.*

27. *The Spaniards in Their History.* Translated by Walter Starkie, New York: Norton, 1950, p. 175.

28. Américo Castro. *De la edad conflictiva,* I. El drama de la honra en España y en su literatura. Madrid: Taurus, 1961, 221 pages. See also H. Th. Oostendorp, *El conflicto entre el honor y el amor en la literatura española hasta el siglo XVII.* La Haya, Van Goor Zonen, 1962.

29. Alfonso García Valdecasas. *El hildalgo y el honor,* Madrid: Revista de Occidente, 1958. Second Edition.

30. See M. Françon, "Sur le sonnet du sonnet," *Modern Language Notes,* LXVII (1952), 46–7, for reference to Voiture's imitation of this sonnet and its ancestor by Diego de Mendoza: "Pedís, reina, un soneto . . ."

31. For further information, see Charles David Ley, *El gracioso en el teatro de la península* (Siglos XVI–XVII). Madrid: Revista de Occidente, 1954; J. H. Arjona, *Hispanic Review,* VII (1939), 1–21; and José F. Montesinos, "Algunas observaciones sobre la figura del donaire en el teatro de Vega," *Homenaje a Menéndez Pidal,* Madrid, 1925, I, pp. 469–504.

32. Rudolph Schevill, *op. cit.,* p. 76.

33. *El sembrar en buena tierra,* A Critical and Annotated Edition of the Autograph Manuscript, by William L. Fichter. New York: Modern Language Association of America; London: Oxford University Press, 1944.

### Chapter Four

1. *La Arcadia* is accessible, but without explanatory notes, in the *Biblioteca de Autores Españoles,* Madrid, Rivadeneyra, 1872 *et seq.,* Vol. 38, pp. 45–136.

2. Carlos Vossler. *Lope de Vega y su tiempo.* Revista de Occidente, Madrid, 1940, second edition, pp. 168–170.

3. See "Lope de Vega's *Peregrino* Lists," by S. Griswold Morley,

## Notes and References

*University of California Publications in Modern Philology,* XIV (1930), No. 5, pp. 345–66; also *The Golden Tapestry,* by B. J. Randall, Durham, N. C.: Duke University Press, 1963, p. 102–12.

4. The title page of the facsimile edition of the Spanish Royal Academy reads *La Dorotea,* acción en prosa de Frey Lope Félix de Vega Carpio del hábito de San Juan . . . año 1632, en Madrid (1951). Other editions are by José Manuel Blecua, Ediciones de la Universidad de Puerto Rico, Revista de Occidente, Madrid, 1955; and Edwin S. Morby, Berkeley and Los Angeles: University of California Press, 1958. Both the Blecua and the Morby editions are annotated.

5. *La Dragontea* de Lope de Vega Carpio. La publica el Museo Naval en Conmemoración del III Centenario del Fénix de los ingenios. Prólogo de D. Gregorio Marañón, Burgos, 1935, 2 vols. See also Dorothy Breen, "An Edition of *La Dragontea* . . . ," University of Illinois Abstracts of Theses, Urbana, 1941; and J. A. Ray, *Drake dans la poésie espagnole,* Paris, 1906.

6. Arturo del Hoyo, ed., *El Isidro,* Madrid, 1935; also *El Isidro,* poema castellano de Lope de Vega. Prehistoria del poema. Simbolismo. Madrid, 1935, 18 pages.

7. Alonso Zamora Vicente, *Lope de Vega, su vida y su obra.* Madrid: Editorial Gredos, 1961, page 156.

8. See Lope Félix de Vega Carpio, *Obras Escogidas,* ed. by Federico Carlos Sáinz de Robles, Madrid: M. Aguilar, 1946, 2 vols. *La hermosura de Angélica* is in volume 2, p. 711–933, without notes or aids.

9. For a brief study and excerpts, see Frank Pierce, *The Heroic Poem of the Spanish Golden Age: Selections,* New York—Toronto: Oxford University Press, 1947, pp. 65–90, and the Introduction; select bibliography, pp. 66–7.

10. *Jerusalén conquistada,* epopeya trágica de Lope Felis de Vega Carpio, Familiar del Santo Oficio de la Inquisición. En Madrid, en la imprenta de Juan de la Cueva, Año de M. DC. IX. (Edición y estudio crítico de Joaquín de Entrambasaguas, Consejo Superior de Investigación Científicas, Instituto "Miguel de Cervantes," Madrid, 1951–1954, 3 volumes.) (Volume II, pp. 70–9 of the Entrambasaguas edition reprints consecutively Lope de Vega's summaries of each chapter or "book" of *Jerusalén conquistada.*)

11. *La gatomaquia,* edited by F. Rodríguez Marín, Madrid, 1935; also edited by Agustín del Campo, Madrid, 1948, in the *Biblioteca Clásica Castilla;* available without notes in *Obras escogidas* de Lope de Vega, edited by F. C. Sáinz de Robles, Madrid: Aguilar, 1946, vol. 2, pp. 1449–1504; and vol. 38 of the *Biblioteca de Autores Españoles,* Madrid, 1872 *et. seq.* Rodríguez Marín counted at least twenty

editions printed since the first one in 1634. See also Antonio Iglesias
Laguna, "Bernardino de Albornoz y su antilopesco poema 'La gaticida
famosa,'" *Cuadernos Hispanoamericanos,* LIV (1963), pp. 647–72.

12. Rodríguez Marín, *op. cit.,* p. lxi–lxii.

## Chapter Five

1. See, *e.g., La Dorotea,* edited by Edwin Morby, University of
California Press, Berkeley and Los Angeles, 1958. Morby identifies
153 proverbs in *La Dorotea,* lists them on pages 455–61, and identifies
several hundred phrases and maxims taken by Lope from the Roman
and Greek classics.

# Selected Bibliography

A. BIBLIOGRAPHIES

SIMÓN DIAZ, JOSÉ, Y JOSÉ PRADES, JUANA DE. *Ensayo de una bibliografía de las obras y artículos sobre la vida y escritos de LOPE
DE VEGA CARPIO*. Madrid: Centro de Estudios Sobre Lope
de Vega, 1955. The most exhaustive bibliography of Lope, although noncritical. The compilers published a supplement to the
above volume entitled *Nuevos estudios, adiciones al Ensayo de
una bibliografía de las obras y artículos sobre Lope de Vega
Carpio*, Madrid, C. S. I. C., 1961. 16 pp.

FICHTER, WILLIAM L. "The Present State of Lope de Vega Studies,"
*Hispania*, XX (1937), 327–52. Indispensable.

GRISMER, RAYMOND L. *Bibliography of Lope de Vega*. Burgess-Beck-
with, Inc., Minneapolis, Minn., 1965, 2 vols. Volume I lists over
3000 books, essays, articles, and reviews dealing with the life
and works of Lope; Vol. II lists manuscripts, editions of known
works, collections, translations, and related material.

PARKER, JACK H., FOX, ARTHUR M. *et al. Lope de Vega Studies 1937–
1962*. A Project of the Research Committee of the Comediantes
(Spanish Group Three of the Modern Language Association of
America) in observance of The Quadricentennial Year. University of Toronto Press, 1964. A well-nigh ideal bibliography; critical comments and frequent summaries of items cited. Indispensable.

MCCREADY, WARREN T. *Bibliografía Temática de estudios sobre el
teatro español Antiguo*. Toronto: University of Toronto Press,
1966.

MOREL-FATIO, ALFRED, AND ROUNET, LÉO. *Bibliographie du Théâtre
espagnol*. Paris, n. d. (about 1900). Critically appraises 163
items.

B. PRIMARY SOURCES

AMEZÚA, AGUSTÍN DE G. *Lope de Vega en sus cartas*. Madrid: Academia Española, 1935–43. 4 vols. A principal source of information
and conjecture about Lope's intimate life.

Cotarelo y Mori, Emilio. See Menéndez y Pelayo, M.

Menéndez y Pelayo, Marcelino. *Obras completas de Lope de Vega,* publicadas por la Real Academia Española. Introducción y notas de M. Menéndez y Pelayo. Biografía de Lope por Cayetano Alberto de la Barrera. Madrid: Sucesores de Rivadeneyra, 1890–1913, 15 vols.; contains drama only, in spite of the title; this collection is far from complete, nor is the continuation of the series by Emilio Cotarelo y Mori, Madrid, 1916–30, 13 vols. Texts offered are sometimes unsatisfactory. There is no edition of the complete works of Lope in existence.

Vega, Lope de. *Colección de las obras sueltas, así en prosa como en verso.* Madrid, 1776–79, 21 vols. Lope's nondramatic writings; not complete. Whenever available, I have made use of annotated editions of Lope's plays, too numerous to be listed here; for information about them, see the Lope bibliographies above, especially Parker-Fox, *Lope de Vega Studies, 1937–1962,* and Robert B. Brown, *Bibliografía de las comedias históricas, tradicionales y legendarias de Lope de Vega,* Mexico, Editorial Academia, 1958. In the United States an increasing number of candidates for the doctorate in Spanish edit plays by Lope in partial fulfillment of the requirements for the degree.

E. Juliá Martínez. *Obras dramáticas escogidas.* Madrid: Biblioteca Clásica, 1934–36, vols. 266–71. (Texts carefully reproduced from the autographs. Contains complete table of contents of the Spanish edition of Lope.)

*Jerusalén conquistada,* epopeya trágica, edición y estudio crítico de Joaquín de Entrambasaguas. Madrid: Consejo Superior de Investigaciones Científicas, 1951–54, 3 vols. One of Lope's efforts to give Spain a great epic poem.

*La Dorotea,* acción en prosa. . . . Madrid: Real Academia Española, 1951. A facsimile without notes of the 1632 edition of Lope's novel in dialogue form; contains numerous incidents based on his personal life. There are several modern editions of *La Dorotea;* the latest is by Edwin S. Morby, University of California Press, Berkeley and Los Angeles, 1958, fully annotated.

*La Dragontea.* Madrid: Museo Naval, 1935, Vol. I. (not published until 1941). Prologue by D. Gregorio Marañón. Originally conceived as a three-volume project; only Vol. I appeared. Volume III, which was to contain the maritime vocabulary of Lope, was lost during the Spanish Civil War of 1936–39. See edition by Dorothy Reeves Breen, unpublished doctoral dissertation, University of Illinois, 1936.

*La gatomaquia,* poema jocoserio . . . primera edicion anotada por

Francisco Rodríguez Marín. Madrid: C. Bermejo, 1935. Annotated.

*Rimas humanas y divinas* del Licenciado Tomé de Burguillos . . . por Frey Lope Félix de Vega Carpio. Madrid: La Imprenta del Reyno, 1634. (Recent facsimile edition; no date, no place.)

*Lírica religiosa de Lope de Vega. Rimas sacras.* Edición facsimilar y estudio de Joaquín de Entrambasaguas. Madrid: Consejo Superior de Investigaciones Ciéntificas, 1963.

*Cardos del Jardín de Lope.* Sátiras del "Fénix," editadas por Joaquín de Entrambasaguas. Madrid, Consejo Superior de Investigaciones Científicas, 1942. A small book, 63 pp., containing recently discovered "thistles," or *cardos*, from the verse of Lope. These verses are grossly worded insults.

*Flor nueva del "Fénix."* Poesías desconocidas y no recopiladas de Lope de Vega. Edición de Joaquín de Entrambasaguas. Madrid: Consejo Superior de Investigaciones, 1942. Recently discovered poems.

*Rimas.* Lope de Vega. Edición y prólogo de Gerardo Diego. Madrid: Palabra y Tiempo, 1963.

*Pastores de Belén.* Lope de Vega Carpio. Madrid, 1675; also Barcelona, Juventud, 1941; 1962.

*La Circe. Poema.* Lope de Vega. Edited by Charles V. Aubrun and M. Muñoz Cortés. Paris: Chefs-d'oeuvres des Lettres Hispaniques, no. 2, 1962, pp. LXXVIII, 96.

*Isidro.* Lope de Vega. Madrid, 1935. (A facsimile of the Madrid, 1599 edition.)

*An Edition of La hermosura de angelica of Lope Félix de Vega Carpio with Notes and an Introductory Essay.* J. B. Burner, Ph.D. thesis, University of Illinois, 1930–31; see also F. C. Sáinz de Robles, *Obras escogidas* de Lope de Vega, Madrid, Aguilar, 1946, Vol. II, pp. 711–933.

*La Arcadia.* Lope de Vega, *Biblioteca de autores españoles.* Madrid: Rivadeneyra, 1872 *et seq.,* Vol. 38, pp. 45–136. (No explanatory notes.)

*Obras dramáticas escogidas* de Lope de Vega, edited by Juliá Martínez. Madrid: Biblioteca Clásica, 1934–36, Vols. CCLXVI–CCLXXI. (These texts are quite faithful to the autographs of Lope.)

Sáinz de Robles, Federico C., editor, *Obras Escogidas,* Lope Félix de Vega Carpio. Madrid: M. Aguilar, 1946, Vol. I, plays; Vol. II, poetry, prose, novels. Convenient thin paper edition, with 3688 pages; offers valuable indices and other information in appendices, but no explanatory notes.

*Comedias Escogidas* de Frey Lope de Vega Carpio, juntas en colección y ordenadas por don Juan Eugenio Hartzenbusch. Madrid: *Biblioteca de autores españoles;* numerous editions; exhaustively indexed; Lope's secular plays are in Vols. 24, 34, 41, 52; his religious plays, Vols. 58, 157. This collection contains a number of faulty texts.

## C. SECONDARY SOURCES

### Biographies

ASTRANA MARÍN, LUÍS. *Vida azarosa de Lope de Vega.* Barcelona: Editorial Juventud, 1941. Second edition, corrected and enlarged from the first, 1932; both editions somewhat novelized.

————. *Lope de Vega, el monstruo de la naturaleza.* Madrid: Imprenta Samarén, Ediciones Bebé, 1944. (I have not seen this volume.)

BAEZA, JOSÉ. *Lope de Vega*—Vida y obra del genio relatadas a los jóvenes. Barcelona: Ediciones Araluce, 1962, 3rd edition. A seminovelized and somewhat apologetic biography written especially to edify Spanish-speaking youth.

BARRERA Y LEIRADO, CAYETANO ALBERTO DE LA. *Nueva biografía de Lope de Vega,* in *Obras de Lope de Vega,* Madrid: La Real Academia Española, 1890, Vol. I.

CABEZAS, JUAN ANTONIO. *Lope de Vega.* Madrid: Nuevas Editoriales Unidas, Madrid, 1962: Part I, biography; Part II, brief anthology; Part III, Lope's epoch.

CASTRO, AMÉRICO. See Rennert, H. A., below.

CARAYON, MARCEL. *Lope de Vega.* Paris: Rieder, 1929. Brief and reliable.

CORREA CALDERÓN, E., AND LÁZARO, FERNANDO. *Lope de Vega y su época.* Madrid, Salamanca: Ediciones Anaya, S. A., 1961. Volume I, *Vida y obra del Fénix;* Vol. II, *Estudio especial de El villano en su rincón.* Volume I offers a 140 page study of the life and times of Lope; Vol. II contains the text of the play noted above, thoroughly footnoted; pp. 165–89 contains a thorough study and analysis of the play. There are a few pages of Lope's lyric poetry, with notes, 190–203. These two volumes are especially prepared for students.

ENTRAMBASAGUAS, JOAQUÍN DE. *Vivir y crear de Lope de Vega.* Madrid: Aldus, 1946, Vol. I. Written by one of the most prolific Lope scholars of the twentieth century.

————. *Vida de Lope de Vega.* Madrid: Editorial Labor, 1942. Reprint of 1936 edition. Entrambasaguas says in *Vivir y crear de*

*Lope de Vega*, p. 3, that this little book was printed without his supervision and contains errors avoidable today.

LAPLANE, GABRIEL. *Lope de Vega*. Paris: Hachette, 1963. A biography well written, with French perspective.

PÉREZ DE MONTALVÁN, JUAN. *Fama posthuma a la vida y muerte del Doctor Frey Lope Félix* . . . Madrid: Imprenta del Reino, 1636. Useful in spite of excess of panegyric, but must be used with caution.

RENNERT, HUGO ALBERT. *The Life of Lope de Vega* (1562–1635), Glasgow, 1904. Reprinted by G. E. Stechert and Co., New York, 1937. Heavily documented standard reference; written primarily for the specialist. Translated into Spanish with modifications by Américo Castro: *Vida de Lope de Vega* (1562–1635), Madrid, Imprenta de los Sucesores de Hernando, 1919. Castro indicates in his foreword the modifications and additions he made in the Spanish edition.

SÁINZ DE ROBLES, FEDERICO CARLOS. *Lope de Vega—Retrato horóscopo, vida y transfiguración*. Madrid: Espasa-Calpe, 1962. Dr. Sáinz de Robles declares on pp. 12 and 13, "I have read carefully and thoroughly everything that has been written about Lope . . . I declare myself to be more than anything else an outright writer—that is, poet rather than critic. Consequently, I feel no obligation whatsoever to submit to the rigorous shackles of orthodox erudition."

VOSSLER, CARLOS. *Lope de Vega y su tiempo*. Madrid: Revista de Occidente, segunda edición, 1940. One of the most highly regarded interpretations of Lope written outside of Spain. Originally published in German: *Lope de Vega und sein Zeitalter*. München: C. H. Beck, 1932: translated by Ramón Gómez de la Serna, Madrid, Revista de Occidente, 1933.

ZAMORA VICENTE, ALONSO. *Lope de Vega, su vida y su obra*. Madrid: Editorial Gredos, 1961. Written with care and sobriety; rich in plot synopses.

D. TRANSLATIONS

Few works of Lope de Vega have crossed the language barrier into English, and even those scarce few are difficult to come by. Below is a brief list of titles restricted to those works fairly easily available.

The most exhaustive list of English translations from Spanish up to the year 1943 is Remigio Ugo Pane, *English Translations from the Spanish 1484–1943*, a bibliography. New Brunswick: Rutgers University Press, 1944. Lope, pp. 195–97.

BARNSTONE, WILLIS, translator. *The Outrageous Saint (La fianza satisfecha)*, *Tulane Drama Review*, VII (1962), 58–104. A prose translation. Barnstone considers the protagonist of this play, Leonido, an existential hero who searches for self-discovery by embarking upon a wild journey of immorality leading to rape, matricide, incest, murder, etc. In the end Leonido is saved when Christ appears to him in person. Leonido dies on a cross repentant. Angel Valbuena Prat calls Leonido "a Freudian character": see *Tulane Drama Review*, VII (1962–63), pp. 44–55.

BOOTY, JILL, translator. *Five Plays* (of Lope de Vega). Introduction by R. F. D. Pring-Mill. New York: Hill and Wang, 1961. Translation made by one who knows the Spanish language well and the stage from personal experience.

CAMPBELL, ROY, translator. *Fuenteovejuna*, in *The Classic Theatre*, edited by Eric Bentley. Garden City, New York: Doubleday and Co., 1959, Vol. III, 161–231. A truly classic translation into verse which stands as a model and a challenge to all future translators of Lope's works.

DUNN, ALBERT H. *The Gardener's Dog (El perro del hortelano)*, Lope de Vega. Translated into English and set to music by A. H. Dunn and B. S. Glagolin. Washington, D. C., 1948.

FLIGELMAN, FRIEDA. *The Discovery of the New World by Columbus*, by Lope de Vega. Translated into English. Berkeley, California: Gillick Press, 1950, 62 pp. A prose translation.

FLORES, ANGEL. *Spanish Drama*, edited and with an introduction. New York: Bantam Books, 1962: *Fuenteovejuna*, pp. 33–80; translated by Angel Flores and Muriel Kittel.

HAYDEN, PHILIP M., translator. *The Star of Seville (La estrella de Sevilla)*, by Lope de Vega. In Brander Matthews, *The Chief European Dramatists*. Boston: Houghton-Mifflin Co., 1916, pp. 167-92. Translated into somewhat stilted English prose.

HAYDN, HIRAM, AND JOHN CHARLES NELSON, editors. *A Renaissance Treasury*. Garden City, New York: Doubleday and Co., 1953, pp. 245–51. Anonymous translation of a story of illicit love and murder from Book One of Lope de Vega's *The Pilgrim*.

JONES, WILLIS KNAPP, translator. "The Rape of Helen" (*El robo de Elena*), by Lope de Vega. In *Spanish One-Act Plays in English*. Dallas, Texas: Tardy, 1934, pp. 92–101. A farce with some passages translated in verse.

JONES, WILLIS KNAPP, translator. *The Stupid Lady (La dama boba)*, by Lope de Vega. *Poet-Lore*, LVII (1962), 291–354.

MATTHEWS, JAMES BRANDER. *Papers on Playmaking*. New York: Hill and Wang: Mermaid Dramabooks, 1957. Contains a translation of Lope's *New Art of Play Writing.*

PANE, REMIGIO UGO. *English Translations from the Spanish: 1484–1943.* A bibliography. New Brunswick, N. J.: Rutgers University Press, 1944. vi, 218 pp. Lists 2,682 items. Lope de Vega: p. 195–197.

PRICE, EVA R., translator. *Peribáñez.* Redlands, California: Fine Arts Press, 1938.

THOMAS, HENRY. *The Star of Seville.* A drama in three acts and in verse attributed to Lope de Vega. Translated out of the Spanish into English verse. Newtown, Montgomeryshire: Gregynog Press, 1935, xiii, 108 pp.

TURNBULL, ELEANOR L. *Ten Centuries of Spanish Poetry:* An Anthology in English Verse with Original Texts from the 11th century to the Generation of 1898. With an Introduction by Pedro Salinas. Baltimore: Johns Hopkins Press, 1955, xv, 452 pp. Offers some verse of Lope de Vega.

UNDERHILL, JOHN GARRETT. *Four Plays by Lope de Vega* in English versions with an Introduction and a critical essay by Jacinto Benavente. New York: Charles Scribner's Sons, 1936, 385 pp. Contains: *A Certainty for a Doubt, The King the Greatest Alcalde, The Gardener's Dog,* and *Fuente Ovejuna.* Translated into rather stilted English; many passages are in verse.

WEATHERLY, E. H., WAGENER, A. P., ZEYDEL, E. H., and YARMOLINSKY, ABRAHAM, editors. *The Heritage of European Literature.* Boston: Ginn and Co., 1948. Vol. I: "The King the Greatest Alcalde" (*El mejor alcalde, el rey,* by Lope de Vega).

E. BOOKS (Other than biographies: Preference is given to items written in English in so far as practicable.)

ADAMS, FRANCIS OSBORNE. "Some Aspects of Lope de Vega's Dramatic Technique as Observed in His Autograph Plays." Unpublished Ph.D. dissertation, University of Illinois, 1936. Lope dipped enormously into universal as well as into Hispanic themes in search of subject matter for his works.

ARCO Y GARAY, RICARDO DEL. *La sociedad española en las obras dramáticas de Lope de Vega.* Madrid: Real Academia Española, 1941. 928 pp. Spanish society in the day of Lope de Vega as he reflects it in his plays.

BARRERA Y LEIRADO, CAYETANO ALBERTO DE LA. *Catálogo bibliográfico y biográfico del teatro antiquo español. . . .* Madrid: Rivadeneyra, 1860. XIII, 724 pp. An indispensable listing of Spanish plays; begins with earliest drama and comes down to the middle of the eighteenth century.

BRENAN, GERALD. *The Literature of the Spanish People*. Cambridge: Cambridge University Press, 1951. Highly readable.

CHANDLER, RICHARD E., AND SCHWARTZ, KESSEL. *A New History of Spanish Literature*. Baton Rouge, Louisiana: Louisiana State University Press; 1961. Part 3 offers an over-all view of the development of Spanish drama.

ENTRAMBASAGUAS, JOAQUÍN DE. *El Madrid de Lope de Vega*. Madrid: Instituto de Estudios Madrileños, 1959. 23 pp. Brief guide with illustrations and maps.

GOLDEN, HERBERT H. *Modern Iberian Language and Literature*. A Bibliography of Homage Studies. Cambridge: Harvard University Press, 1958.

HURTADO, JUAN, AND GONZÁLEZ-PALENCIA, ANGEL. *Historia de la literatura española*. Madrid: Saeta, 6th edition, 1949. 1102 pp. A standard handbook.

*La casa de Lope de Vega*. Real Academia Española. Madrid: Atlas, 1962. 186 pp. See also pamphlet, *La casa de Lope de Vega*, issued free by the Publicaciones de la Dirección General del Turismo, Madrid; and *La casa de Lope de Vega*, por Pedro Muguruza Otaño, arquitecto, en Madrid, Diciembre de MCMXLI, issued by the Real Academia Española.

MARÍN, DIEGO. *La intriga secundaria en el teatro de Lope de Vega*. México: Ediciones de Andrea (University of Toronto Press, Toronto), 1958. According to the Parker-Fox bibliography, "a monograph of highest value." It contains analyses of 146 authentic plays of Lope for convenient reference.

MENÉNDEZ Y PELAYO, MARCELINO. *Estudios sobre el teatro de Lope de Vega*. Santander: Aldus, 1949. 6 vols. The "Edición Nacional" of the complete works of Menéndez Pelayo. A standard reference.

MÉRIMÉE, EARNEST, AND MORLEY, S. GRISWOLD. *A History of Spanish Literature*. New York: Henry Holt and Co., 1930. Brief study of Lope de Vega in Chapter IV.

MORLEY, S. GRISWOLD, AND BRUERTON, COURTNEY. *The Chronology of Lope de Vega's Comedias*. New York: The Modern Language Association of America (London, Oxford University Press), 1940. Indispensable. For additional information on chronology of Lope's plays, see *Hispanic Review*, XV (1947), Schevill Memorial Number.

NORTHUP, GEORGE TYLER. *An Introduction to Spanish Literature*. Chicago: University of Chicago Press, 1960 (3rd edition, revised by N. B. Adams). See chapter on "Lope de Vega and His Dramatic School."

PARKER, A. A. *The Approach to the Spanish Drama of the Golden Age*. London: The Hispanic and Luso-Brazilian Councils, 1957. 27 pp. A formulation of five principles of dramatic construction which Parker offers as necessary for better comprehending seventeenth-century Spanish drama. Reprinted in the *Tulane Drama Review*, IV (1959), 42–59.

PARKER, JACK HORACE. *Breve historia del teatro español*. México: "Manuales Studium," 1957. Vol. 6. Brief handbook, numerous references.

PAVIA, MARIO N. *Drama of the Siglo de Oro*. Study of magic, witchcraft, and other occult beliefs. New York: Hispanic Institute, 1957.

RANDALL, DALE B. J. *The Golden Tapestry*. A critical survey of non-chivalric Spanish fiction in English translation (1543–1657). Durham, N. C.: Duke University Press, 1963. See pp. 102–12 for information on Lope's *El peregrino en su patria* in England, translated anonymously as *The Pilgrime of Casteele* in 1621 and considerably altered for the English reader.

RENNERT, HUGO A. *The Spanish Stage in the Time of Lope de Vega*. New York: Hispanic Society of America, 1909. Reprinted minus the "List of Spanish Actors and Actresses, 1560–1680," by Dover Publications, New York, 1963. Indispensable.

SHOEMAKER, WILLIAM H. *The Multiple Stage in Spain During the Fifteenth and Sixteenth Centuries*. Princeton: Princeton University Press, 1935. A scholarly Ph.D. dissertation. Indispensable.

TICKNOR, GEORGE. *History of Spanish Literature*. Boston, 6th edition, 1888. A standard reference.

TRUEBLOOD, ALAN S. "Substance and Form in 'La Dorotea.' A Study in Lope's Artistic Use of Personal Experience." Unpublished Ph.D. dissertation, Harvard University, 1951.

VALBUENA PRAT, ANGEL. *Literatura dramática española*. Madrid, Barcelona: Editorial Labor, 1930; 2nd edition, 1950. Illustrated. Chronological evolution of Spanish drama from its beginnings.

F. BIOGRAPHICAL AND CRITICAL ESSAYS: Preference is given to items written in English in so far as practicable.

ARJONA, J. H. "La introducción del gracioso en el teatro de Lope de Vega," *Hispanic Review*, VII (1939), 1–21. A documented study of the indispensable seventeenth-century comic.

ARJONA, J. H. "Modern Psychology in Lope de Vega," *Bulletin of the*

*Comediantes,* VIII (Spring, 1956). A *gracioso,* or comic, Mendo by name, tells how he "conditioned" cats in an experiment which he describes to his listeners. The experiment was based on the principle that learning is the formation of conditioned responses, the same principle followed by I. W. Pavlov in his experiment performed upon dogs centuries after Lope. Mendo is a character in *El capellán de la Virgen.* In Lope's *El castigo sin venganza,* another comic enumerates phobias, obsessions, and compulsions universally felt although not admitted until modern psychology took away from them the taboo of serious abnormalities. Arjona says, "A careful scrutiny of Lope's plays would reveal many more instances in which he foreshadowed our modern psychological findings." See also W. A. Bousfield, "Lope de Vega on Early Conditioning," *American Psychologist,* X (1955), 828.

FUCILLA, JOSEPH E. "Finea in Lope's *La dama boba* in the Light of Modern Psychology," *Bulletin of the Comediantes,* VII (Fall, 1955), No. 2, p. 22. The protagonist, a young girl named Finea, manifests a pseudo-stupidity of which she is cured by the devotion of her lover: on pseudo-stupidity, see Maslow and Mittleman. *Principles of Abnormal Psychology.* New York: Harper's, 1941, pp. 543–46.

GILDER, ROSAMOND. "Lope de Vega, Super Man of the Theatre," *Theatre Arts Monthly,* XIX (1935), 660–85.

HALSTEAD, FRANK G. "The Attitude of Lope de Vega Toward Astrology," *Hispanic Review,* VII (1939), 205–19. Well-documented study.

HAYES, FRANCIS C. "The Use of Proverbs as Titles and Motives in the *Siglo de oro* Drama: Lope de Vega," *Hispanic Review,* VI (1938), 305–23.

HAYES, FRANCIS C. "The Collecting of Proverbs in Spain Before 1650," *Hispania,* XX (1937), 85–94. Interest in proverbs ran high in Lope de Vega's Spain.

JAMESON, A. K. "Lope de Vega's Knowledge of Classical Literature," *Bulletin Hispanique,* XXXVIII (1936), 444–501.

JAMESON, A. K. "The Sources of Lope de Vega's Erudition," *Hispanic Review,* V (1937), 124–39. Highly critical of Lope's thought, asserting that Lope showed no profundity, read and accepted what he found without reflection.

LEAVITT, S. E. "The Popular Appeal of Golden Age Drama in Spain." University of North Carolina Extension *Bulletin,* XXVIII (1949), No. 3, pp. 7–15.

LEONARD, IRVING A. "Notes on Lope de Vega's Works in the Spanish Indies," *Hispanic Review,* VI (1938), 277–93. Offers evidence of Lope's popularity in the New World. Contrary evidence, at least for Peru, is offered by Guillermo Lohmann Villena in *El arte dramático en Lima durante el Virreinato*. Sevilla: Universidad de Sevilla, 1945.

McCRARY, WILLIAM C. "Fuenteovejuna: Its Platonic Vision and Execution," *Studies in Philology*, LVIII (1961), 179–92. Building on the studies of others, McCrary argues that *Fuenteovejuna* is a "reconstitution of history according to the canons of a normative Platonic vision."

McCREADY, WARREN T. "Lope de Vega's Birthdate and Horoscope," *Hispanic Review*, XXVIII (1960), 313–18. Timely proof that Lope's birthdate was December 12 rather than November 25 as stated by Pérez de Montalbán, Lope's first biographer.

PEERS, E. ALLISON. "Mysticism in the Poetry of Lope de Vega," *Estudios dedicados a Menéndez Pidal*, Madrid, 1950, Vol. I, pp. 349–58. "Lope was as unmystical a religious poet as his age produced," concludes Peers.

POESSE, WALTER. "Disertaciones lopescas: Una compilación," *Hispanófila*, No. 18 (Mayo, 1963), pp. 77–89. Lists edited editions of plays as well as Masters' and Doctors' theses.

PRING-MILL, R. D. F. "Sententiousness in *Fuente Ovejuna*," *Tulane Drama Review*, VII (1962), 5–37. The conclusions drawn about the great sententiousness of *Fuenteovejuna* hold for many other plays of Lope and his contemporaries.

REICHENBERGER, ARNOLD G. "The Uniqueness of the *Comedia*," *Hispanic Review*, XXVII (1959), 303–16. An excellent analysis.

SALOMON, N. "Sur les représentation théâtrales dans les 'pueblos' des provinces de Madrid et Tolède (1589–1640)." *Bulletin Hispanique*, LXII (1960), No. 4. On Spain's small-town theaters in the time of Lope de Vega.

SCHEVILL, RUDOLPH. "Erasmus and the Fate of the Liberalistic Movement Prior to the Counter Reformation," *Hispanic Review*, V (1937), 103–23. Pages 119–20 deal with Spanish drama; Schevill's thesis is that "the creation of a stereotype pattern of social conduct and thought is most apparent. . . . In hundreds of *comedias* a dominating conformist character in plot and idea can be verified. . . . With the destruction of Erasmian inquiry, dogmatic authority replaced question and speculation."

WARDROPPER, BRUCE W. "On the Fourth Centenary of Lope de Vega's Birth," *Drama Survey*, II (1962), 117–29.

WILDER, THORNTON. "Lope, Pinedo, Some Child Actors and a Lion," *Romance Philology*, VII (1953), 19–25. Shows keen perspicacity in dating 19 plays of Lope. See also Courtney Bruerton, "Thornton Wilder and Lope's *Peregrino* Lists," *Bulletin of the Comediantes,* III (1951), No. 1, p. 1.

WILSON, WILLIAM E. "Contemporary Manners in the Plays of Lope de Vega," *Bulletin of Hispanic Studies,* XVII (1940), 3–23, 88–102. Informative study of customs.

# Index

All titles in English are followed by their original title in Spanish and the name of their author. Lope Félix de Vega Carpio is abbreviated to Lope.

# Index

# Index